Naming
Your
GOD

Naming Your GOD

THE SEARCH FOR MATURE IMAGES

Pat McCloskey, O.F.M.

AVE MARIA PRESS   Notre Dame, Indiana 46556

Nihil Obstat: Rev. Hilarion Kistner, O.F.M.
Rev. Christopher R. Armstrong

Imprimi Potest: Rev. Jeremy Harrington, O.F.M.
Provincial

Imprimatur: + James H. Garland,
Auxiliary Bishop of the Archdiocese of Cincinnati,
15 February 1989

The *Nihil Obstat* and *Imprimatur* are official declarations that a book or pamphlet is free of doctrinal or moral error. No implication is contained therein that those who have granted the *Nihil Obstat* and *Imprimatur* agree with the contents, opinions or statements expressed.

International Standard Book Number: 0-87793-452-5

Library of Congress Catalog Card Number: 90-85157

Cover and text design by Katherine Robinson Coleman.

Printed and bound in the United States of America.

Contents

For all people "wandering between two worlds"
regarding their images of God.
May they experience God's love
and the support of friends.

Introduction

I suppose this book has been in the making since the day I heard the confession of a woman who asked pardon for the miscarriage she had suffered fifty years before. She was probably at least seventy years old (she was behind the screen), and after she had recounted the circumstances of the miscarriage, which was not due to any negligence on her part, I tried to assure her that she had committed no sin and that God perfectly understood her situation and indeed wanted her to forgive herself. I suspect she accepted that intellectually, but I do not know if that changed anything for her emotionally. God knows how many times she had already asked forgiveness for that supposed sin. I remember thinking to myself, what kind of a God has she been worshipping all these years? What kind of baggage from that tragedy had she been carrying for the last half century? How many other people have been carrying similar baggage?

That incident came back to me when I saw Roland Joffe's movie "The Mission." Mendoza, the repentant slave trader (Robert DeNiro), accompanies Father Gabriel (Jeremy Irons) and several other Jesuits up the steep Iguazu Falls, lugging his armor, the symbol of a life Mendoza has left behind, a life where he killed his own brother in a lover's triangle. The former slave trader has dragged this armor for miles as penance for that sin, and when the other Jesuits urge Father Gabriel to end the penance, he replies that the time is not yet ripe. At the top of the falls the Guarini Indians, whom Mendoza had once hunted, are waiting to welcome the Jesuits. Tension rises when they see Mendoza, but finally a young boy steps forward with a machete, pauses, and then cuts the rope; the net with the armor falls back into the river. Mendoza feels a tremendous sense of relief and is generously welcomed by the Indians. The entire sequence conveys a sense of baptismal cleansing and reconciliation.

Often we drag along behind us images of God—and related images of ourselves and others—that are increasingly heavy. Yet we refuse to leave them behind because we fear that new images might be even heavier in the sense of requiring an even greater conversion on our part. Unlike the movie, where someone else could decide that Mendoza did not have to carry that burden any longer, only we can decide to accept new images of God, self, and others. Try as they may, other people can only challenge our images, point out self-contradictions, and encourage us to convert, to discover more adequate, more generous, more truthful images about all three. No one else can cut the rope that binds us to images we do not fully trust yet are unwilling to leave behind. The images of God we may be dragging around with great weariness are the same images that, whether we intend it or not, we are conveying to others.

In this book the phrases *my God* and *your God* indicate only a person's perception of God—not the total reality of God. For better or for worse, we act on the basis of our perceptions. We can perceive danger where there is none (a creaking door on a stormy night), or we can be oblivious to danger where it exists (a build-up of carbon monoxide gas). Our perception of a situation may be mistaken, but we will always act on the basis of that perception—until we realize that we have misunderstood the situation. We can compare our understanding of a situation to someone else's perception of the same situation ("Do you feel cold? No? Maybe I'm coming down with something").

We often discuss political candidates and programs in order to compare our perceptions with those of others. We may talk to friends, watch TV debates, read newspaper or magazine articles, or check the literature from the League of Women Voters.

Regarding personal problems we may talk to a friend, clergyperson, or therapist to sort out puzzling or conflicting feelings about relationships. At times an entire family may go for group counselling to untangle the family members' perceptions and misperceptions. For example, group intervention may be necessary if a chemically dependent person is to perceive accurately what is happening to him or her—and to friends and family members.

What is true of personal or family relationships is also true of our relationship with God. Our perceptions may be accurate, or we may be misinterpreting the evidence, but in any case, we will act on the basis of those perceptions until we decide they are incomplete and that accepting new images is less risky than acting on the old ones.

I have identified my sources and listed other books and tapes to help readers interested in a particular issue find additional resources for continuing reflection and decision. At the end of each chapter I have included questions to aid private prayer and reflection. Groups interested in images of God, self, and others, and their interrelation, will find questions to help them face those images and their consequences. I hope everyone will find here some new information and, even more important, the encouragement to step back and review his or her images of God, self, and others—and then begin to make any necessary changes.

ONE

Is Your God Too Small?

Some months after my book *When You Are Angry With God*[1] was published, I received a letter from a woman who had read it and wanted to know if God was lying when the Bible says to pray for those things we need. Her father-in-law had never accepted her marriage; for three years she remembered this man at Mass, during novena devotions, and when she prayed the rosary. She prayed that her father-in-law would accept this marriage and her friendship. No change. To make matters worse, her father-in-law had recently died and was buried before she or her husband were informed—and then by a friend! The deceased man had wanted it that way. Now face-to-face reconciliation was impossible this side of heaven.

This letter writer did not sound to me as though she wanted to meet her father-in-law in the life beyond this one! She cited Jesus' words:

> Ask, and it will be given to you; search, and you will find; knock, and the door will be opened to you (Mt 7:7).

Then she wrote, "Well, Father, I asked for my father-in-law's friendship, and what did I receive? Dogshit. Why did I bother? What did I expect?"

11

After recounting her experience of telephoning a Christian radio station and being told she expected too much from God—an answer she considered unsatisfactory—she asked if she had misunderstood the above passage from Matthew's gospel, and if so, what else in the Bible had she—and others—misunderstood? Why did God require Christ's death on the cross? "Is God so high that this is the only thing that will satisfy him?" she wrote. "Apparently he is!" Then she added:

> I can't read of God's answering other people's prayers in magazines or listen to such stories on the radio, because it didn't work out that way with me. I think "Good for you, but I'm not you. I was lied to! I thought God had made me his daughter, but apparently I am not correct."

Perhaps her problem, she finally concluded, was that she did expect too much of God after all. Maybe it would be better to skip the rosary and novenas and stick with the Serenity Prayer:

> Lord, grant me the serenity to accept the things I cannot change, the courage to change the things I can, and the wisdom to know the difference.

"Then if God says no," she wrote, "I don't have the memory of how I 'prayed always' and 'prayed believing.' If God loves me, why do I have to go to all that trouble? I had better results when I did the best I could and left the rest up to God—God answered my prayers better when I bothered him less!"

Readers of these lines may say that this letter writer had several mistaken perceptions—that prayer guarantees a desired outcome, that God the Father required Christ's death on the cross because that was the only way Christ could atone for sin, and that the letter writer was not God's daughter—but she clearly was acting on the basis of her perceptions and would undoubtedly continue to act on them until she accepted more truthful images of God, herself, and others.

Her letter reminds me of the scene in the Book of Judges where the Hebrews are oppressed by the Midianites.

> The Angel of Yahweh appeared to [Gideon] and said, "Yahweh is with you, valiant warrior!" Gideon replied, "Excuse me, my lord, but if Yahweh is with us, why is all this happening to us? And where are all his miracles which our ancestors used to tell us about when they said, 'Did not Yahweh bring us out of Egypt?' But now Yahweh has deserted us; he has abandoned us to Midian" (Jgs 6:12–13).

The oppression suffered by Israel was very real to Gideon; the sense of rejection felt by the letter writer was equally real. Gideon was able to put God to the test twice (one night dew fell all around a fleece; another night dew fell only on the fleece but not on the ground), and eventually Gideon led the Israelites to a great victory against the Midianites. The letter writer, on the other hand, felt that God failed the test and was not helping her conquer the situation.

For me, the most chilling lines of her letter were in the last part: "God answered my prayers better when I bothered him less." I'm afraid that a God who can't be bothered will eventually be worshipped by someone who can't be bothered either. What begins as a problem with God's seeming unresponsiveness to prayers of petition will probably end in isolation from other believers, frozen bitterness, and an incapacity to offer those in pain any better answer than "you think you've got problems? Let me tell you what happened to me."

Part of my answer to this woman was recalling my own experience of praying for my two nephews, who were born two months prematurely, lived for a few days and then died. I was almost seventeen when this happened, and my world turned upside down—as this woman's did—by a difficult family situation that could not be healed face-to-face this side of heaven. She felt betrayed, that her prayers had been worthless. I too had felt betrayed when my nephews died, and I had to re-assess what my prayers of petition meant and to what kind of God I was addressing them. "Quite simply," I told her, "you misunderstood what God meant by the words 'ask and you will receive'—just as I did when my nephews died."

I related to her the story Rabbi Harold Kushner tells of the ten years he spent dealing with his son's progeria, a rare but always fatal illness that ages a person prematurely. The disease killed Aaron Kushner two days after his fourteenth birthday. In *When Bad Things Happen to Good People*, Rabbi Kushner says that we can redeem tragedies such as this from senselessness by imposing a meaning on them. "The question we should be asking," he says, "is not, 'Why did this happen to me? What did I do to deserve this?' That is really an unanswerable, pointless question. A better question would be, 'Now that this has happened to me, what am I going to do about it?' " Later he says:

> The facts of life and death are neutral. We, by our responses, give suffering either a positive or a negative meaning. Illnesses, accidents, human tragedies kill people. But they do not necessarily kill life or faith. If the death and suffering of someone we love makes us bitter, jealous, against all religion, and incapable of happiness, *we* turn the person who died into one of the "devil's martyrs" [witnesses against God].[2]

I encouraged the letter writer to talk to a fellow parishioner whom she respected and who had dealt with great suffering. Perhaps she could ask why that person didn't simply quit believing in God or what sustained him or her in the most difficult moments. I explained that I don't think any of us can deal adequately with life's sufferings by gritting our teeth and carrying on alone. The community has its faults, but God's self-revelation always involves a community. We recognize the Bible as the word of God because the Christian community tells us it is. If we misunderstand part of the scriptures, it's the community that tries to help us get it straight. And it's the community that helps us grow in compassion as the good Samaritan did.

Perhaps my answer to this woman helped her see personal suffering from a more biblical perspective, but perceptions like hers are not easily changed. Though neither of us explicitly mentioned our personal challenges to faith (her relationship with her father-in-law and the death of my nephews) in terms of our images of God, those images were and are basic to resolving both situations. Images of God we acquire at an early age may cause problems later unless we can see both the truth and the limitations of those images.

Images of God

Don't fix it if it's not broken, we say. I believe that most of us gravitate toward one or two images of God that help us make sense of life around us. For example, God is a loving creator who may not answer my selfish prayers—like winning the lottery—but who will certainly answer my prayers if the issue is more serious—like someone's life. At least that was one of my images of God—until the day my two nephews died.

But if I have a single image of God, and this image is decisively contradicted by my new and painful experience of life (God will always protect me, but last week I was beaten and robbed for the first time), I have the same options, in a sense, as if I outgrow a pair of shoes: 1) I can continue to wear the same shoes and complain that they do not fit (Why is this good God punishing me?); 2) I can quit wearing shoes altogether (become an atheist or an agnostic); or 3) I can find shoes that fit. The final option forces me to seek out additional images of God that do justice to *all* of life as I have experienced it. If I am a Christian and I choose that option, I will probably have to re-examine the scriptures and the lives of Christians to see if I have missed some key information. In fact, the third option is a commitment to continual growth in my images of God—with immediate consequences for my self-image and my image of others.

In one sense life is easier if I have a single image of God. When Job lost his wealth, sons, and daughters and then became deathly sick, three friends came to comfort him. Yet they insisted on maintaining an image of God that said such tragedies are always a punishment for sin. The only solution they could see was for Job to admit his sin and ask God's pardon. Once upon a time Job must have shared that same image of God, but in his sickness he moves beyond it because he sees that his "tit for tat" morality is not working. Job's friends are scandalized, but Job boldly questions God's justice and says he wants to go to court with God and have an impartial judge hear the case. By the end of the Book of Job, the image Job's friends had of God has been discredited. God is angry with Job's friends "for not having spoken correctly about me as my servant Job has done" (Jb 42:7). Job did not set out to change his image of God, but when his sufferings began, Job refused to accept the image of God offered by his friends. He insisted on a better explanation. In effect, God praised Job's painful and prayerful search, a search that led him to more mature images of God. Job's friends then had to retire and, we hope, retrace their steps theologically to see where they had gone wrong. They needed to grow in their images of God.[3]

Have Your Images of God Grown?

Imagine that when you were five years old someone asked you to describe your parents. Perhaps you would have answered (or did!) that your mother was very loving (the world's best cook), your father was very strong (more so than your friend's father), and that together your parents took very good care of you. Now imagine that at age thirty you were asked the same question. Would you simply repeat your earlier answers? Hardly. Although you might use some of the same words (strength, love, care), they would have a deeper meaning.

Which description of your parents would be the correct one—the one you gave at age five or at age thirty? Is it possible that they are both correct and are simply reflections of your growing ability to appreciate your parents?

It would be a mistake to disregard the five-year-old's description of his or her parents or to accept it as the last word. Important discoveries, both positive and negative, await the person willing to see the "whole picture." Perhaps, for example, you admired your father for being able to handle every situation, but later you realized that this ability had a "shadow" side; what looked heroic to you as a child may seem ruthless when you become an adult.

Or perhaps you thought your mother was very ordinary (unlike someone else's mother), and later you

realized that your mother's "ordinariness" was quite remarkable: dependable, hard-working, faithful love.

Over the years the traits we admire in a person may
appear in a new perspective—either positive or negative. It is, of course, possible to remain frozen in our
earliest impressions of our parents. As a result, we may
idealize them, never allowing them to become real people with their own difficulties and "shadows," or we
may fail to see good qualities we didn't value properly
when we were children. If we can act this way with
our own parents, why should we be surprised to find
that our childhood images of God are insufficient? Is
God insulted that we didn't understand everything correctly from childhood? Or does God regret that as adults
we are content to rely exclusively on those childhood
images?

God was not pleased that Job's friends would deny
what they saw, an innocent man suffering, rather than
rethink their image of God to include both the suffering
of the innocent and the total providence of God. Refus-
ing to accept the cold, heartless God his friends describe,
Job seeks a God who can give some meaning to such suffering. Thus, in his suffering Job grows in his images of
God. If Job had accepted the advice of his friends, he
would have betrayed God, himself, and everyone else
whose life touched his. When our previous images of
God contradict what we know to be true, we can complain perpetually (Why is this happening to me?), quit
believing in God, or seek other images of God that do
justice to our experience and to God's self-revelation in
the scriptures.

Isn't That Cheating, Making God in Your Own Image?

"Wait a minute," you may be saying. "That's cheat-
ing. You can't construct an image of God to explain all
your problems or disappointments in life. You're mak-

ing God in your own image—rather than being made in God's image."

Not at all. A God tailor-made to suit the purposes of an individual or group quickly becomes an idol to be destroyed. However, God has chosen to use a great variety of words and images to reveal himself. Many people use exclusively male imagery about God, but we know that God is neither male nor female. In Chapter 7, I will present this issue as a potential area for group conversion regarding our language about God. The God of Abraham, Isaac, and Jacob, the God of the Exodus from Egypt and the Exile into Babylon, the God of the prophets and the psalmists, the God revealed as Trinity in the New Testament, this God is never fully understood by any words or images human beings may use.

If my images of God have been quite satisfactory for some time but are now called into question by my present experience (If God is good, why is this happening to me?), why should I refuse to consider that my images of God may be too confining—for God and for me?

Idolatry, making a physical object and worshipping it as a god, may also mean accepting one particular image of God to the exclusion of all others. For example, the expression *Christian racist* ought to strike us as a contradiction in terms, but there are people who would deny that contradiction. They may see God as a master planner, arranging all creation in a very orderly way and establishing their race as the master of all others. I won't deny that God is a master planner and has arranged creation with great order, but I do deny the application that a Christian racist may draw from those two facts. Such a person may feel that he or she has a completely adequate image of God, but *thinking that does not make it so.* The same person might describe any other image of God as a betrayal of the biblical heritage, but it would be far easier to show that the Christian racist has betrayed God's self-revelation as contained in the scriptures.

Several years ago the evening news showed a group of Christian leaders peacefully marching on the South African federal legislature. With bibles in hand these leaders were taken away by the police and later released. That same news program showed footage of another march held shortly before, a demonstration in which supporters of apartheid (the great majority of them Christian!) complained that the government was being too conciliatory with the non-white population (the majority) in South Africa.

Both sides believe in the Bible; both sides call themselves Christian; both sides say that the soul of South Africa is at stake in this conflict. The two sides, however, certainly do not have identical images of God. Apartheid supporters speak of the order God put in the universe—meaning that God put them in charge. Apartheid opponents speak of the dignity of all women, men, and children created by God—meaning that apartheid is an insult to God as well as to his sons and daughters.

There are many forms of idolatry, many ways of making God extremely neat, tidy, and supportive of our own self-interest; all of them "domesticate" God to the point where the person who accepts one image or rejects another is in total charge. Such idolatry protects some self-interest without appearing to do so.

Orthodoxy: The Real Issue?

Orthodoxy (concern with correct belief and correct practice) can be a real issue in a conflict between persons or groups, or it can be a smoke screen, a useful way of confusing the situation and not allowing the real issue to surface.

Job's friends felt that their explanations about God were orthodox and that Job was denying the basics of their faith and of his. Though they begin pleasantly, they end harshly when Job rejects their "cruel comfort" and insists on challenging God in order to receive a satisfactory explanation of what has happened to him. Indeed, Job was denying a basic tenet of their faith (all suffering is a consequence of a person's sin). Job was on the verge of seeing a blind spot in that faith; God was operating in a way Job's friends refused to see.

Religious orthodoxy can be mature or premature. By the end of the story Job's orthodoxy was mature. He knew that all suffering is *not* a result of a person's sins, that God does not send suffering in order to test people's faith. His friends realized that their previous orthodoxy had been zealous but premature; that is, it was unwilling to reconsider the evidence and was concerned only for protecting itself.[4] The Book of Job closes with the central figure offering a sacrifice for the sins of his three friends, who previously had been sure they understood the fundamentals of their faith but are now struggling to understand how they had mistaken a peripheral matter for a fundamental of faith, and vice versa.

A premature orthodoxy uses God as a weapon to bolster one's own position. The worst of the Pharisees in the New Testament—and not all of them were petty, self-righteous people—used their scrupulous observance of the Law as a way of establishing their authority and dominating others.[5] For them, anyone who did not observe the Law as they understood it was a sinner. Remnants of that attitude remain. Consider the following story.

For his book *American Dreams: Lost and Found*, Studs Terkel interviewed many people, including Peggy Terry, a woman born in the hills of western Kentucky. She had

worked at various jobs around the country and then
became a leader of poor southern whites in Chicago's
Uptown section. Reflecting on her grandmother's poor
self-image, Peggy says:

> My grandmother was a real wonderful person,
> so full of joy, but she carried this terrible bur-
> den with her. They call this being under convic-
> tion. You're under conviction when you feel you
> have done terrible sins. She couldn't have sinned
> that bad—she was too poor. [Peggy laughs.] The
> Church made them feel guilty. They're so bur-
> dened down, and it tells them they're nobody.
> Don't look for anything here on earth. The day
> you die, you're gonna get all those things you
> didn't get while you were living. It took me thirty
> years to fight my way out of that. I thought I was
> nothing.[6]

Peggy Terry's grandmother probably felt that by accepting this sense of being "under conviction" she was being
faithful to the fundamentals of Christianity. But was she?
Or was she a victim of someone else's attempt to domi-
nate and manipulate in the name of religion, in the name
of speaking the last word about God's will?

There is a mature orthodoxy, which I will try to
explain in greater depth in Chapter 6, but for now I
think it is enough to say that we will probably never
understand the real thing unless we realize that it has
imitators. Everything that glitters is not gold, and everything that proclaims itself as orthodoxy is not the
real thing. We may not like to hear Peggy Terry's criticism of the Christian group she knew best, but can we
say that her experience is unique? How many people
think that they can be honest adults only by throwing
off the guilt-ridden humility they think God requires?
Would Job have been a more faithful believer if he had
accepted the kind of humility preached by his friends?

No, if my previous images of God are now challenged by my present experience (cancer, death of a good friend, crippling car accident), I am showing good spiritual health if I question those previous images. If someone suggests that my questions are inappropriate and challenging God's will, I may back down, but does that solve anything? Does that help me to love God, myself, and other people any better? Will that make me a better witness to the good news Jesus came to preach and live?

A Deepened Faith or a Deadened Faith?

Every personal crisis brings our images of God to the forefront. Life cannot be the same afterward. Even if I outwardly accept God's will as the explanation for what happened, I cannot be the same as before—not in the way I perceive God, myself, or other people. Another story may help here.

In December 1984 Sister Suzanne Schrautemyer went to a doctor because of a lump under her right arm. When the lump was found to be malignant, she underwent a partial mastectomy and six weeks of radiation treatment. The following year she discovered a lump under her other arm. It too was malignant, and so she had a bilateral mastectomy and a round of chemotherapy. In the early summer of 1986 she discovered another lump under her left arm, and tests showed that cancer had spread to her bone marrow. At the age of thirty-nine Sister Suzanne decided to accept her coming death and discontinue chemotherapy.

Prior to that decision she went through several months of low-grade anger and depression; she had difficulty talking about this with anyone. "I had to be assured it's okay to be angry, to doubt, to be broken and down," she said. "I don't believe now that my faith is insulted by my anger and doubt. I had to move through it—those real human experiences—before I could let go of it."

When she told the sisters in her community about her decision to discontinue chemotherapy, they felt angry and depressed. "I told them I needed them to be real. If they were angry at me for being sick again, that's okay, I said. If they're angry at God because I might be dying, that's okay. And it's okay to show that to me. I told them I wanted them—and I needed them—to be real."

Had her faith changed during that two-year ordeal? "Yes, it's simpler," she responded. "I used to think some places, people, times were more sacred than others. My experience of faith now tells me that everything, every moment is sacred. Everything that happens is a sacrament, a moment when God becomes tangible and life is real. That's what's different."[7]

For every person like Sister Suzanne, whose faith has deepened as a result of questioning God in the face of a fatal illness, there are others whose faith has been deadened by the experience. Some sufferers make a noisy exit from their practice of religion, but many others may continue identifying with a particular group of believers, yet without much conviction—as Job probably would have done if he had accepted his friends' advice. Perhaps he would have decided that God, responsible for the whole universe, cannot be bothered with the problems of individuals. Or perhaps in an attempt to discover the personal sin that caused this suffering—his friends had said it was there somewhere—Job would have become obsessed with observing the smallest details of the Law. If so, he might have overlooked the more fundamental elements like justice and mercy—as Jesus said the Pharisees did (see Mt 23:23). In trying to observe God's law Job might have become imprisoned in a progressively smaller world of his own making. One's willingness to re-examine previous images of God can be the difference between a deepened faith and a deadened faith.

Where to begin? Speaking from a Christian perspective, I believe that our images of God are often related to our childhood impressions from the Hebrew scriptures. However, although the basic stories may be familiar, these books offer far more information about God—fuller images—than many Christians suspect. The following chapter will try to present some of the richness and variety of those books.

For Personal Reflection

1. Do I have images of God that I neither fully trust nor am willing to leave behind? What prevents me from letting go of those images?
2. Have I ever prayed for something very important and then felt betrayed by God at the outcome?
3. Have I been seriously tempted to quit believing in God? Was any one person helpful during my faith crisis? What did that person say or do?
4. What are my dominant images of God? Have I come to these as a result of individual or communal challenges to faith?
5. What do I mean by the expression *God's will*? Do I use it more readily to describe other people's suffering than my own?

For Group Discussion

1. What images does the expression *the God of the Old Testament* evoke for you? With which stories are those images most closely connected?
2. Some people might say that if prayer does not change a situation, at least it should change the praying person's perception of the situation. What do you say?
3. What do you think of Rabbi Kushner's statement that the

facts of life and death are neutral, and that by our response
we give suffering a positive or a negative meaning?

4. Does our sense that God is in charge make us uncomfortable when people like Job ask angry questions? How can
we deal with such feelings?

5. If we had been members of Sister Suzanne's community
when she said it was okay to be angry with God because
she was dying, how would we have reacted? How would
we have felt?

Further Resources

Andrew Greeley, *The Religious Imagination* (New York: William
H. Sadlier Inc., 1981).

Martin Lang, *Acquiring Our Image of God* (Mahwah, NJ: Paulist
Press, 1983).

John B. Philipps, *Your God Is Too Small* (New York: Macmillan
Publishing Co., Inc., 1953). Part One demolishes thirteen
unreal images of God; Part Two presents an adequate,
focused image of God.

TWO

Images of God in the Hebrew Scriptures

Map makers have a fairly easy time depicting well-known lands. If you look at a map of Europe made 600 years ago, you will see Greece and Italy depicted as peninsulas, Great Britain as an island, and the coastline of North Africa fairly well represented. European map makers believed that they were representing the civilized world; the rest was labelled *terra incognita* (unknown territory). Other cultures have likewise tended to see themselves as the apex of civilization.

Those who draw the maps and assign the names tend to assume that the *terra incognita* is monotonously the same and so are its inhabitants. It's easy to say, "They're all alike" if a person has never known one of "them" personally, much less as an equal.

For the majority of Christians, aren't most of the Hebrew scriptures *terra incognita*, a breeding ground for gross generalizations that gloss over the diversity of viewpoints within those inspired writings? This tendency reduces thousands of years of history and theology into a single unknown. But didn't all the Old Testament writers have the same social, political, and theological interests? Not at all. Here, as elsewhere, the truth is both more complex and much more rewarding than quick generalizations.

Granted, most Christians are familiar with at least one of the creation stories (there are two), with the story of Adam and Eve's idyllic existence in the garden, their disobedience and expulsion, the story of Noah and the ark, several stories about Abraham, especially the near-sacrifice of his son Isaac, the stories about the Exodus, the covenant at Mount Sinai, the fall of Jericho, and several stories about King David. Based on this acquaintance, Christians often feel justified in portraying the God of the Hebrew scriptures as a jealous, angry God surrounded by thunder and lightning, inclined to wage war and to keep very accurate records about who has observed the Law of Moses and who has not. Although all these images find some support in the Hebrew scriptures, its *total* revelation of God is much more complex and enriching. All that wealth, however, goes to waste if people assume that their single image of God in the Hebrew scriptures is "the real thing."

A thousand years ago a European map maker could hardly be faulted for not knowing how far south the continent of Africa extends; that North, Central, and South America lie to the west; and that Asia is the largest continent. But even when exploration improved the knowledge of geography, people were not always anxious to discard faulty information and replace it with more accurate but more complex information. Generalizations make the world much more simple, saving a lot of time and energy.

Sweeping generalizations about the Hebrew scriptures may likewise save time and energy. Unfortunately, such ignorance is always costly. If we gloss over the hundreds of years during which the Hebrew scriptures were written, when the very different images of God used by the inspired writers were developed, we jeopardize our ability to see God acting in human history, including our own history.

As the Hebrew scriptures become less and less *terra incognita* for us, we can begin to appreciate the diversity present in writings we may have thought were all the same. Between the covers of our bibles we have almost two thousand years of God's self-revelation (Abraham to A.D. 100), plus a priceless explanation of how the world came to be, why human beings were created, and how sin entered into the world. The Bible is a library containing many different types of books; we err if we act as if those books were all the same—each author sharing the exact same concerns and agreeing with every other author in all matters. This diversity is there for a reason, and all of it has been accepted as inspired by God. If we are content with sweeping generalizations about "God in the Old Testament," who is the loser? We are.

Images of God in the Pentateuch

Three Traditions in Genesis

The Book of Genesis is well-known in the sense that most Christians are familiar with the stories of Adam and Eve, Cain and Abel, Noah, the Tower of Babel, Abraham, Isaac, Jacob, and Joseph. Yet many Christians are surprised to learn that the Book of Genesis combines three literary and theological traditions, not all with the same image of God; that the story of the creation of the world in seven days is only one of two creation stories; that Genesis contains many doublets, stories told twice and from quite different viewpoints[1]; and that the Book of Genesis might not have been the first book of the Hebrew scriptures to reach its final form.

In 1753 Jean Astruc published a book suggesting that the Book of Genesis does not come from a single author but is a compilation of distinct literary and theological traditions. Researchers eventually accepted this theory and called these traditions the Yahwist, the Elohist, and the Priestly accounts. The Yahwist and Elohist are so named because they use different names for God. The Priestly account reflects an interest in genealogies and correct liturgical observance.

Not all Jews and Christians welcomed these theories about literary and theological traditions in Genesis; some people saw this whole line of thinking as a way of emphasizing the "humanness" of Genesis and thus denying the truth of its revelation about God.[2] Was this part of a rationalist plot to reduce the scriptures to amusing folk tales? How can the Bible be inspired if within the same book (traditionally ascribed to Moses as author) there are quite distinct literary and theological traditions? Besides, isn't it terribly presumptuous to suggest that researchers in the eighteenth and nineteenth centuries discovered three literary traditions in Genesis when saints and scholars had been studying the book for centuries without coming to that conclusion?

Yahwist Tradition: A Personal and Vivid God. The oldest of the three literary traditions in Genesis, and probably the first one to reach its final written form, is called Yahwist because Yahweh is God's personal name and is used as such in one of the creation stories. During the ninth or tenth century B.C., the Yahwist tradition began as an oral tradition and was probably finalized in the Southern Kingdom. In 931 B.C. the policies of King David's grandson split the kingdom into North (ten tribes) and South (tribes of Judah and Benjamin).

The Yahwist stories tend to be very vivid, the dialogues very engaging. The author readily applies human characteristics to God; for example, God has hands and feet and can feel joy and anger. However, these anthropomorphisms do not make Yahweh simply a magnified version of a human being, as the Greek gods often are. The advantages and risks of applying human characteristics to God are described in the Appendix.

The Yahwist tradition is interested in the wide sweep of history. There is a consistent preference for the younger son (Isaac/Ishmael, Jacob/Esau, Judah/older brothers), and an interest in showing how God prepared the way for King David to establish a great dynasty. The Yahwist author gives us the older of the two creation accounts: God forming the first man from clay and breathing life into this clay; God then creating the trees and all the animals; man naming all the animals but finding no partner; the first woman formed from the rib of Adam; the story of Adam, Eve, the serpent, and the forbidden fruit; the expulsion from the garden; the story of Cain and Abel. These vivid stories are told from the Yahwist point of view. The Yahwist tradition appears again in the Book of Exodus and in the Book of Numbers.

The Yahwist tradition presents a "hands-on" God who fashions the first man from clay, breathes life into him, creates the first woman, makes marriage an exclusive commitment, banishes Adam and Eve for their disobedience, and holds Cain accountable for the murder of Abel. When people speak of God in the Old Testament as severe and aloof, they are overlooking the Yahwist tradition. God honors human beings by giving them freedom, taking them seriously, and offering them ways to be in communion with their Creator.

Elohist Tradition: A Distant but Involved God. The second oldest tradition in the Book of Genesis is called Elohist because it uses a more generic name for God,

Elohim. This Hebrew word is plural and can be applied to pagan gods or to the one true God, in which case the corresponding verb is singular. The Elohist tradition uses the term in both senses. This tradition may date from the eighth century B.C. in the Northern Kingdom. The narrative style is less vivid and tends to stress the distance between God and human beings; God is totally unlike any of his creatures. Rather than speak directly (for example, to Adam, Cain, and Noah), God prefers to reveal himself through dreams and visits from angels (such as Jacob's vision of the angels on a stairway or Joseph's ability to interpret dreams).

The Hebrew scriptures contain several stories that often trouble modern readers, who have difficulty believing that God would act as the stories suggest (for example, the angry God who destroyed most of the human race through the flood or killed all the non-Hebrew first-born in Egypt). Perhaps no story is more troubling than the one about the near-sacrifice of Isaac (Gn 22:1–9), which is told predominantly from the Elohist point of view.

What kind of God is presented in the story of Isaac? The editors of the *New Jerusalem Bible* say that this account illustrates

> the difference between an Israelite shrine, where human sacrifice did not take place, and Canaanite ones where it did. The story as it stands justifies the ritual prescription for the redemption of the first-born of Israel: like all "first-fruits" these belong to God; they are not, however, to be sacrificed but bought back, "redeemed," Ex 13:12. Lying behind the story, therefore, is the condemnation, so frequent in the prophets, of child-sacrifice, see Lv 18:21.[3]

In *A Path Through Genesis* Bruce Vawter writes:

> The sacrifice of a human being, so repugnant to
> us and with such difficulty associated with a di-
> vine command, would not have appeared too
> strange to Abraham. There is no evidence that
> human sacrifice was ever practiced by the He-
> brews, but it was common among the Canaanites
> with whom Abraham lived, and how was he to
> know that God, the ruler of life, would not re-
> quire this thing of him?[4]

Perhaps the preceding explanation puts a new light on the story and modifies our image of God. Abraham's readiness to obey and his fear of God are praised. Abraham had no point of reference that said child sacrifice was an abomination; we have that point of reference partly because this story is told about Abraham. The God of Abraham, Isaac, and Jacob is a God deeply involved in human history; he does not toy with human beings as pagan gods so often do. There are limits to what God will ask, and child sacrifice is one of them. God abhors child sacrifice. This story conveys that information very effectively.

The Elohist tradition suggests that God is not infinitely "chummy." Moral standards are important. This tradition arose as a way of supporting belief in one God at a time when some Israelites had accepted the polytheism of their neighbors and were ready to see the God of Abraham, Isaac, and Jacob as one of many gods. The Elohist image of God may seem very severe to us, but how else does one combat the temptation to add the God of the patriarchs to a long list of other gods? How else does one challenge the less strict moral standards that Israel's polytheistic neighbors followed?

Priestly Tradition: A God of Order and Creation.   The Priestly tradition is so named because the author has a great interest in details about sacrifices offered, historical events that explain liturgical practices, and genealogies.

Whereas the Yahwist and Elohist traditions presume that sacrifices can be offered in various places, the Priestly tradition identifies the Jerusalem Temple as the only lawful place to offer sacrifice. This tradition tends to avoid anthropomorphisms and can be rather abstract or redundant; it probably reached its final form during the Exile in Babylon (587–538 B.C.) when many Jewish people were trying to figure out how this nation so blessed by God could have its Temple destroyed and be reduced to being governed by pagans.

The better-known creation account (six days of work and then God rested) is from the Priestly tradition; one of its aims is showing that the sabbath rest has been part of God's plan for the world from the very beginning. The Priestly tradition allows itself a rare anthropomorphism in order to emphasize the divine approval of the sabbath rest. Against pagan creation myths, which saw the world as resulting from conflict between the gods, the Priestly account stresses that all of creation comes from a single source and that in its natural state every created thing is good. The genealogy from Adam to Noah and God's covenant sealed with a rainbow are credited to the Priestly tradition—likewise the covenant of circumcision. The Priestly tradition overlaps the Yahwist tradition in several stories about Esau, Jacob, and Joseph. The Book of Genesis probably reached its final written form after the Exile in Babylon; the Priestly editor interwove the three literary and theological traditions.

Deuteronomic Tradition: The God of the Covenant

The fourth major literary and theological tradition in the Pentateuch is called Deuteronomic from the Greek words for "second law." This tradition has roots in the Northern Kingdom but became influential in the Southern Kingdom during the seventh century B.C.

This literary and theological tradition emphasizes that out of pure love God has chosen Israel to be his special people, not because of its greatness and power but simply because God loves it. The key event in this tradition is the covenant between God and the Hebrews at Mount Sinai. The Law given to Moses is the guarantee of that covenant; Israel observes that Law as a response to its election by God: "If you are really prepared to obey me and keep my covenant, you, out of all peoples, shall be my personal possession" (Ex 19:5).

In the time of the patriarchs, sacrifice could be offered in various shrines and by various people; according to the Deuteronomic tradition sacrifice can be offered only in Jerusalem and only by members of the priestly tribe. The Deuteronomic tradition has a strong sense of urgency; the expressions "you, today, now" link its present audience to their ancestors at the time of the Exodus. This tradition received its final written form after the return from Exile in Babylon, after the Hebrews had concluded that their nation had been reduced to domination by pagans because the kings of Israel and later of Judah had betrayed the Sinai covenant.

The Deuteronomic tradition helped shape post-Exilic Judaism by stressing the Law as its central point of reference. Even after the Temple was rebuilt and sacrifices could be offered there, the Law remained central to Jewish self-identity because the Law could be observed even by Jews who lived far from Jerusalem and could visit the Temple only once a year or once every few years. Scribes (men learned in the Law) and synagogues (places of prayer and study of the Law) became an increasingly important part of Jewish identity.

If we understand the Deuteronomic tradition as its authors understood it, we see a faithful God loving a people whose allegiance is often halfhearted, a people sometimes severely tempted to worship other gods or to borrow religious practices from their pagan neighbors, a people who did not witness the Exodus and the Sinai covenant and whose primary contact with those mighty deeds of God is through the Law.

Observing the negative commandments indicates only the rough boundaries of God's revelation—not how the person lives within those boundaries as a faithful son or daughter of the covenant. According to the Deuteronomic tradition God does not love the Israelites because they keep the Law. Rather, God loves them when they do not merit it, when they are not even a people possessing their own land. The people respond to that free choice by God, to that absolutely unmerited love, by keeping the Law in loving obedience. If one is not careful about the sequence of events, however, keeping the Law can become the explanation for God's love of his Chosen People. But that is not what the Deuteronomic tradition says. This basic sequence

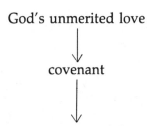

God's unmerited love

↓

covenant

↓

Law as an expression of the covenant

is often confused in the history of Israel and later in Christianity, with immediate and disastrous consequences.

But This Is Only a Theory!

"Yahwist, Elohist, Priestly, Deuteronomic! Scholars may find these terms interesting," you may be saying, "but the average person who reads the Bible couldn't care less. And besides, this is all theory." Granted. However, each literary/theological tradition has a distinct image of God, with very practical consequences for one's self-image and image of others. The average person who reads the Bible may find one of those images of God very comfortable but may be threatened by the others.

What happens, for example, if I accept the Yahwist image—God as very approachable—in a distorted way? God could seem to be a "pal," with all the strengths and weaknesses of any human friend. God might be bargained with, encouraged to endorse my cozy view of the world, and even bribed through prayer if necessary. What began as a distorted image of God quickly leads to a mistaken self-image (God's buddy) and image of others (some, but not all, are also God's buddies).

The person who feels energized only by the Elohist image of God could end up with an extremely aloof and severe God who speaks through individual dreams and visions but never through group prayer and reflection. Such an image of God easily lends itself to self-deception and haughtiness toward others. People who speak negatively of "God in the Old Testament" often take the Elohist image of God out of context. Catholic and Protestant fundamentalists tend to use this image exclusively.

If I distort the Priestly image of God, order and custom can become more important than God. Liturgical observance can become an end in itself rather than a way of praising God. I can see myself as a good person if I observe certain rituals—regardless of any inner conversion. I may judge other people on their zeal for the rituals I consider important.

If I misunderstand the Deuteronomic tradition, my image is distorted. I see a God who lays down heavy

burdens through the Law and offers little help to carry
them, a God who gives great detail in liturgical and di-
etary regulations but may not seem terribly interested in
the other parts of life, a God who approves of legalism
and observing only the externals of religion.

So, each of the literary/theological traditions in the
Pentateuch can be distorted. If I identify myself with one
tradition and dismiss the others, my life will become
more simple as my images of God, myself, and others
fall into place. But will my life be more truthful? If God
inspired such diversity, perhaps those diverse images of
God are not supposed to fall into place quite so easily.
If each tradition is inspired, then each one has something important to teach us—even if we more naturally
gravitate to one than to the others.

The theory about the four literary and theological
traditions used in the Pentateuch does much to explain
internal contradictions, repetitions, and sometimes jarring chronological order. But perhaps even more valuable is its variety of images of God. Within each tradition
there is the possibility of a distorted view of God; it is
the final product of these four traditions we recognize as
inspired—not one tradition to the exclusion of the others. Shouldn't we try to understand that diversity with
its immediate and practical consequences for how we
pray to God, how we see our lives, and how we see
other people?

Images of God in the Historical Books

The Historical Books include the books of Joshua,
Judges, Samuel, Kings, Chronicles, Ezra, Nehemiah,
Ruth, Tobit, Judith, Esther, and Maccabees. Most of these
books cover events between the covenant at Mount Sinai
(c.1250 B.C.) and the return of the Jews from Babylon
(538 B.C.).

In their final form, therefore, these books are the product of a school, of a number of devout men profoundly influenced by the outlook of Deuteronomy, men who meditated on the history of their nation and extracted a religious lesson from it. At the same time they hand on an account of the outstanding events in the history of Israel and traditions or texts that date back to the heroic age of the Conquest. From these books the believer will not only learn to see the hand of God in all world events, but in God's exacting love for his chosen people will recognize the slow preparation for the New Israel, the community of the faithful.[5]

Of course, we cannot exclude a feminine contribution to the Deuteronomic tradition as well; for example, in the Book of Judges the prophetess Deborah judges Israel.

Joshua: A Warrior God

In the Book of Joshua we meet a God who stands behind the capture and annihilation of the pagan peoples in the Promised Land, a God who requires a holy war to complete the deliverance from Egypt by settling the Israelites in their own land. The central figure of Moses is replaced by his assistant Joshua, and this holy war is presented as an extended act of worship, of faithfulness to the Sinai covenant. Although the Book of Joshua makes the conquest sound continuous, complete, and without setback, the Book of Judges shows that it was not so simple. Both books emphasize that the Israelites must avoid contamination by the religious beliefs and practices of their pagan neighbors.

Many modern readers wince when they see that the Book of Joshua demands that all the pagans in the cities conquered by the Israelites must be killed. Was all that bloodshed God's will? Joshua tells the people that Yahweh is a jealous god who will not tolerate their misdeeds or sins. If they desert Yahweh, he will destroy them.

The image of God presented in the Book of Joshua is drawn with very sharp strokes, which its intended audience would immediately understand. The disobedience of Achan, who steals some of the spoils, results in the death of his sons and daughters; all the spoils of war belong to Yahweh; if the people desert Yahweh, they will be destroyed. A particular culture sometimes limits God's self-revelation in the same way that a child's level of maturity limits a parent's possibility of self-revelation. The Book of Joshua's style is quite understandable in view of the difficulty of maintaining belief in one God in a land where polytheism and related moral practices were previously the norm. The later books of Samuel and Kings indicate how readily the Hebrews accepted some of their pagan neighbors' customs. The sharp picture drawn in the Book of Joshua is modified in later parts of the Hebrew scriptures—especially the part about a son or daughter bearing the guilt of a parent. In fact, even when many Israelites go back on their ancestors' promise to be God's people, the entire nation is not destroyed; a remnant survives.

The Book of Joshua stresses that God's way is important; it cannot be considered one among various options. We need to make major decisions about the God we serve and the people we are becoming—and then support those general decisions through day-to-day choices.

If our image of God focuses too strongly on the image of the warrior God of Joshua, we may see fighting as our main mission, with God tagging along to bless our battles. When the Germanic tribes became Christian in the fifth to tenth centuries, they understandably were attracted to the image of God in the Book of Joshua. In time they learned there was more to Christianity.

Ezra and Nehemiah: A God of Joy and Law

Ezra is called the Father of Judaism because in the fifth century B.C. he shaped three of its dominant features: the sense of being a chosen race, the Temple, and the Law. In doing so he also reshapes the people's images of God. Once Nehemiah has rebuilt the walls of Jerusalem and resettled the area, Ezra assembles the people and reads the Law of Moses (Pentateuch); then the Levites explain it. On hearing the Law and realizing their infidelity, the people begin to cry. Ezra tells the people, "You may go; eat what is rich, drink what is sweet and send a helping to the man who has nothing prepared. For today is sacred to our Lord. Do not be sad: the joy of Yahweh is your stronghold" (Neh 8:10). For a whole week Ezra reads the Law to them and they celebrate; then comes the time for expiation. The people fast, wear sackcloth and ashes and gather to confess their sins while the Levites sing about God's mighty deeds from creation until that very day. Then they promise to observe the Law of Moses and not to intermarry with pagans, to rest on the sabbath, to pay a Temple tax, and bring the first fruits of their crops and the first-born of their sons, their cattle, and their flocks.

Images of God in the Prophets

The Hebrew prophets who wrote the seventeen inspired books named for them lived within a 600-year period of Israel's history. Operating in the Northern Kingdom, Southern Kingdom, in Exile, or in post-Exilic Israel, these prophets came from all levels of society; their writings reveal varying degrees of theological and literary development. We cannot assume that if we

brought all seventeen of them together they would agree
on everything, but we can be sure that the word of the
Lord came to each of them with a message for their
contemporaries and for future generations anxious to
worship the God of Abraham, Isaac, and Jacob. By not
using identical images of God the prophets expand our
ability to speak about God and to see our lives as God
sees them. Indeed, many prophets had to expose the lies
accepted as conventional wisdom and indicate what true
justice, worship, and fidelity to the Lord mean.

Although we usually associate the word *prophet*
with someone who predicts the future, the Hebrews understood prophets as people so filled with the word of
the Lord that they must speak it and proclaim it by symbolic action. Sometimes the prophets threaten; at other
times they describe a nation doing penance. Depending
on the situation of the people, the prophets may console or denounce—all to help form the consciences of
the people.

The Hebrew prophets always denounce idolatry.
Such idolatry can take the crude form of worshipping
wooden or stone idols, but more often it refers to worshipping a God who has become totally domesticated,
for example, a God who is satisfied with precise liturgical observance without any sense of social justice
(Amos). Prophets denounce the way in which God's will
has been perverted; often they foretell the rewards of
a future era in which the divine will has been understood correctly and lived out generously. Even people
who do not worship wooden or stone idols may fashion
for themselves a "cozy" God who leaves them free to
pursue their own plans.

The prophets sought "to keep the nation faithful to
the true religion of Yahweh" and were "instruments especially chosen by God to further divine revelation."[6]

They furthered or developed that revelation in three main areas: monotheism, morality, and future salvation.

A God Who Loves Honest Sacrifices

Amos, a shepherd from Judah and a trimmer of sycamore trees, was sent to the Northern Kingdom to prophesy during the reign of King Jeroboam (783–743 B.C.), a time of considerable wealth and elaborate liturgical celebrations but little concern for social justice. Amos begins with the customary prophecies against neighboring pagan nations, and then he shocks his listeners by adding:

Yahweh says this:

For the three crimes, the four crimes of Israel,
I have made my decree and will not relent (Am 2:6).

Yahweh is going to punish Israel for its injustice toward the poor and the weak. Assyria stands ready as the instrument of God's anger. Concerning their trips to the sanctuaries at Bethel and Gilgal, Yahweh says sarcastically:

Bring your sacrifices each morning,
your tithes every third day,
burn your thank-offering of leaven
and widely publicize your free-will offerings,
for this, children of Israel, is what makes you
happy (Am 4:4–5).

The people apparently love their liturgies, but hate the man who teaches justice at the city gate. Hardened in their sins the Israelites expect God's intervention against their enemies, but again Yahweh speaks:

I hate, I scorn your festivals,
I take no pleasure in your solemn assemblies.
When you bring me burnt offerings . . .

your oblations, I do not accept them
and I do not look at your communion sacrifices
 of fat cattle.
Spare me the din of your chanting,
let me hear none of your strumming on lyres,
but let justice flow like water,
and uprightness like a never-failing stream! (Am
 5:21–24).

Amos presents a more holistic God than Israel
wants to accept, a God who wants liturgical celebrations
to represent a conversion that has already taken place or
is in process. People who pride themselves on worshipping in a royal sanctuary or a national temple may not
be as open to conversion, to a life of prayer and justice,
as they think they are. Against their too-comfortable images of God, Amos' prophecies describe a God who will
punish their injustices and then lead them back to genuine freedom. People who smugly worship God (as did
those addressed by Amos) tend also to be smug about
their own power in relation to other nations. When they
fail in relation to God and to the other nations, we could
say that God punished them, but we could also say
that by making God in their own image they punished
themselves.

Hosea: A Faithful God

Hosea, a contemporary of Amos, prophesied in the
Northern Kingdom as Israel was approaching its annihilation by Assyria in 721 B.C. God commands Hosea
to marry Gomer and to name their elder son Jezreel (literally, "God sows" but also the place where King Jehu
killed King Ahab's wife and children), their daughter
Lo-Ruhamah ("without pity"), and their younger son
Lo-Ammi ("not-my-people"). After God calls Israel an
unfaithful wife and denies that he is her husband, he
begins his lawsuit, the record of God's ardent, faithful

love and Israel's running after other gods.[7] She must remove the signs of her adultery (perhaps amulets of pagan gods) and be stripped naked (the punishment for unfaithful wives). Her children are not God's children.

God plans to frustrate Israel's attempts to rejoin her lovers; only then will she realize that it was God, and not they, who gave her grain, wine, oil, silver, and gold.

Then God says he will seduce Israel, lead her into the desert again and speak to her heart, and there she will respond as she did when she was young, as on the day when she came up from Egypt. She will address God as husband and not as "Baal" (literally, "master," but also the name for a Canaanite fertility god). God will re-establish the harmony of nature and banish Israel's enemies so that she may sleep secure. The symbolic names of Hosea's children will be reversed by God, who will take pity on the people and acknowledge them as his own. Hosea's life and prophecies blend together to an unusual degree.

The prophet Hosea next denounces the priests for profiting from the sin of the people and for not opposing sacred prostitution, part of the Canaanite fertility rites. Foreign alliances and appeals to Assyrian kings will not save the people. When the Israelites begin to repent and seek healing, God says that their love is like "the morning mist, like the dew that quickly disappears" (Hos 6:4). Thus, God will continue to punish them,

> for faithful love is what pleases me, not sacrifice;
> knowledge of God, not burnt offerings (Hos 6:6).

Kings, advisers, and common people are equally depraved and deceived in trusting foreign alliances. The people will be led into exile, their sanctuaries will be destroyed, and thorns and thistles will overrun their altars.

The prophet presents Israel not only as God's wife but as God's son:

When Israel was a child I loved him,
and I called my son out of Egypt.
But the more I called, the further they went away
   from me;
they offered sacrifice to Baal
and burnt incense to idols.
I myself taught Ephraim to walk,
I myself took them by the arm,
but they did not know that I was the one caring
   for them,
that I was leading them with human ties,
with leading-strings of love,
that, with them, I was like someone lifting an
   infant to his cheek,
and that I bent down to feed him (Hos 11:1–4).

Do the other prophets and Hosea have identical images of God, of the way God will deal with Israel's sins?
Not at all. God is revealing himself in all of these diverse images, and the person who has room for only
one image will be the poorer. Hosea's imagery breaks
all previous barriers to show the extent of Israel's sins
and the faithful love of her spouse, God. That image will
be developed in the other prophets and New Testament
writers. Hosea's contemporaries apparently felt that God
was distant and easily satisfied with halfhearted sacrifices; the prophet presents a God passionately in love
with Israel and ready to do whatever is necessary to help
her come to her senses, to repent. The Lord God is not
one member of a heavenly court of gods, all of whom deserve sacrifice; he is Israel's faithful, forgiving husband.

Isaiah: A Holy and Mighty God

The prophet Isaiah began his career around 740 B.C.
in the Southern Kingdom and prophesied approximately
forty years. Either directly or through his disciples he is
the main author of Isaiah 1–39; even so, some of these

chapters (such as 25–27) date from a much later period. Chapters 40–55, called the Book of Consolation, were probably written during the Babylonian Exile by an author now identified as Second Isaiah. Chapters 56–66 might be contemporary with the rebuilding of the Temple and thus may have been written by yet another author, Third Isaiah. Each part of the book makes valuable contributions to our images of God. In this chapter the name Isaiah will refer to the prophet who died around 700 B.C.

Isaiah begins with God's lament that the people have abandoned him, the Holy One of Israel. Holy One is a favorite title for God in this book. The whole nation is sick and prone to offer Temple sacrifices that reflect unconverted hearts.

> "What are your endless sacrifices to me?" says
>   Yahweh.
> "I am sick of burnt offerings of rams
> and the fat of calves.
> . . .
> Your hands are covered in blood,
> wash, make yourselves clean.
> Take your wrong-doing out of my sight.
> Cease doing evil. Learn to do good,
> search for justice, discipline the violent,
> be just to the orphan, plead for the widow" (Is
>   1:11; 15–17).

If the people ask pardon, God will forgive. If not, the sword will come upon them. Perhaps more than any other writer in the Hebrew scriptures, Isaiah conveys a strong sense of God's majesty, of God's glory, which humbles the arrogance of sinners.

Isaiah compares God to the owner of a vineyard, who tends it carefully, expecting it to yield fine grapes, but finds only wild grapes. God asks whose fault this is and resolves to destroy its walls and hedges, allowing it to become overgrown. Other prophets and New Testament writers will develop this image.[8]

Isaiah's inaugural vision describes the Lord as seated on a high and lofty throne, his train filling the sanctuary of the Temple. The six-winged seraphim proclaim, "Holy, holy, holy is Yahweh Sabaoth. His glory fills the whole earth" (Is 6:3). Emmanuel (God-with-us) will come to restore the nation. In this future age, Yahweh will prepare a magnificent banquet to which all the nations will be invited, and they will put their hope in him.

Toward the end of the Jewish Exile in Babylon the prophet known as Second Isaiah begins his mission by citing God's words that he should console Jerusalem and tell her that her guilt has been atoned for, that God in all his glory is about to lead the people back through the desert (a second Exodus) and remain with them.

> He is like a shepherd feeding his flock,
> gathering lambs in his arms,
> holding them against his breast
> and leading to their rest the mother ewes
>   (Is 40:11).

The image of God as a shepherd becomes stronger in later Judaism, especially in Jeremiah, Ezekiel, and Zechariah. Whereas earlier sections in the Hebrew scriptures, such as Joshua, had suggested that other nations have their own gods but Israel must be faithful to the God of the Exodus, Second Isaiah proclaims a stronger monotheism: Those other gods are not gods but statues of wood or stone. Yahweh, the Lord of history, stands ready to use Cyrus, the king of the Persians, as his instrument to deliver Israel from captivity.

The people are to turn back to Yahweh, to a God who is rich in forgiveness. In Second Isaiah we find four songs of the Servant of Yahweh, masterpieces of revelation about God's intention to teach all the nations and sustain his servant (perhaps an individual or the entire nation of Israel) amid the sufferings that often accompany a decision to do God's will.[9] The Lord remains with his people even in their moments of tremendous suffering.

The writer sometimes known as Third Isaiah reasserts God's will to save all peoples who love his name and become his servants. God repeatedly criticizes Israelites whose external worship far surpasses their inner conversion. Yet Jerusalem will abundantly nourish all who come to her, and God will send her peace.

The prophet Isaiah and his successors have left us images of God as majestic, all-holy, forgiving, a generous host, a healer, a shepherd, the Lord of history, strength of the afflicted, and defender of the oppressed. If Isaiah and his successors accepted all these images of God, shouldn't that warn us not to cling to one or two favorite images and ignore the others?

Ezekiel: A Majestic and Compassionate God

The prophet Ezekiel was a priest probably taken to Babylon in the first series of deportations (597 B.C.). He venerates the Law, the Temple worship, and the requirements of legal purity, but emphasizes that people must be interiorly ready when they come to worship.

Ezekiel pictures God in very majestic terms, even describing how the "Glory of God" has left the Jerusalem Temple, which is now polluted with pagan sacrifices and emblems. The Jewish people, a "rebellious tribe," will be severely punished. The phrase "And they will know that I am Yahweh" (*New American Bible*) is almost a refrain for Ezekiel; it appears sixty-seven times in this book. The expression "declares the Lord Yahweh" occurs 201 times.

God, who judges and punishes, will not leave his people desolate; he acts with justice and compassion. But, like the other prophets, Ezekiel reminds us that a superficial repentance will not be sufficient.

Perhaps Ezekiel's teaching on individual responsibility represents his greatest contribution to his contemporaries' images of God—and ours. Whereas God's revelations to Abraham, Moses, and Joshua stressed the whole family as being saved or punished, the prophet Ezekiel emphasizes the importance of each person's decision. Thus if a nation is unfaithful to God, even if Noah, Daniel, and Job, known for their uprightness, were present, "they would be able to save neither son nor daughter, only themselves by their uprightness" (Ez 14:20). By stressing individual responsibility Ezekiel reinforces the idea that a person can indeed repent and thus avoid the condemnation sinning ancestors received. There is no inevitable link in good deeds or in evil deeds; each person has the chance to start afresh or fall into the rut of sin. God says:

> If the wicked, however, renounces all the sins he has committed, respects my laws and is law-abiding and upright, he will most certainly live; he will not die. . . .
>
> But if the upright abandons uprightness and does wrong by copying all the loathsome practices of the wicked, is he to live? All his upright actions will be forgotten from then on; for the infidelity of which he is guilty and the sin which he has committed, he will most certainly die (Ez 18:21–24).

If God acted in any other way, he would be punishing innocent people for the sins of their ancestors and condoning the guilty because of the holiness of their forebears.

Ezekiel also continues and strengthens Hosea's images of God as a faithful husband and Israel as a faithless wife.

Perhaps one of Ezekiel's strongest images for God is that of shepherd. Ezekiel is told to prophesy against Israel's shepherds (kings) who have fed themselves and not looked after the lost, scattered sheep of Israel. Yahweh will intervene and look after the flock himself, bringing them back from the various nations to which they have been scattered. The Lord will raise up a shepherd for them. Ezekiel describes a rebuilt and purified Temple, to which the glory of Yahweh will return and remain while the people rebuild a nation in which the worship of Yahweh will be exteriorly correct and interiorly sincere.

Ezekiel presents a majestic, transcendent God, who nevertheless has compassion on his people and stands ready to help them repent and build a new life, individually and as a nation. God has loved Israel and will shepherd the nation in a totally selfless way. He will breathe on the dry bones of Israel and bring them to life.

Jonah: A God for All People

In some ways the Book of Jonah is like the Book of Genesis: well-known but not fully appreciated. For some people the most memorable part of the book is that Jonah is swallowed by a whale, not that God wants a pagan city to be saved and that, in fact, the people do repent, much to the shock and displeasure of Jonah. All the characters in the story are likeable—except Jonah.[10] With masterful irony the author presents an inspired message about the universality of God's love and the need to repent.

Trying to avoid God's command to preach repentance in Nineveh, Jonah runs away, is caught in a storm, thrown overboard, and swallowed by a large fish. Once

freed, Jonah carries out what he considers a useless task.
These pagans, however, surprise him by accepting his
message of repentance. Then the disgruntled Jonah becomes enraged and says he had foreseen Nineveh's repentance: "I knew you were a tender, compassionate
God, slow to anger, rich in faithful love, who relents
about inflicting disaster" (Jon 4:2). Praying to die, Jonah
goes a short distance from the city and builds himself
a shelter from which he can watch the city. When God
causes a castor-oil bean plant to grow and give shade to
Jonah, the prophet's disposition improves. But then God
sends a worm to attack the plant and it withers, leaving
Jonah unprotected under a scorching sun. Jonah says he
has a perfect right to be angry with God for destroying
the plant, but God responds:

> You are concerned for the castor-oil plant which
> has not cost you any effort and which you did not
> grow, which came up in a night and has perished
> in a night. So why should I not be concerned
> for Nineveh, the great city, in which there are
> more than a hundred and twenty thousand peo-
> ple who cannot tell their right hand from their
> left, to say nothing of all the animals? (Jon
> 4:10–11).

With that emphatic question, the Book of Jonah ends.
      People who insist on the historical accuracy of the
story about the whale and other details of Jonah's story
often miss the main message of the book—that God
is tender, compassionate, slow to anger, rich in faithful love, and willing to relent in inflicting disaster. God
desires not only that Jonah be saved from "the pit" but
that *all* peoples repent and be saved. If the prophets pre-
dict "woes," and the people repent, perhaps that is the
best possible way of "fulfilling" the prophecy. The Book
of Jonah cautions against turning the God of Abraham,

Isaac, and Jacob into a God concerned for the Jews and no one else. He desires the salvation of all peoples.

Images of God in the Wisdom Writings

In very general terms the wisdom writings include the books of Job, Psalms, Proverbs, Song of Songs, Wisdom, Qoheleth (Ecclesiastes), and Sirach (Ecclesiasticus). The Hebrew wisdom writings developed between Solomon (c. 970 B.C.) and the first century before Christ; the oldest parts of this literary and theological tradition show an influence from the wisdom collections of Egypt and Mesopotamia. Although some of the Hebrew wisdom writings predate the Babylonian Exile, most come from the years after the return to Jerusalem.

Wisdom literature was originally concerned with the education of court officials, with instructions about life and individual conduct. Most of the instruction is given in the father/son or teacher/pupil format. Eventually *wisdom* is seen as a common need rather than the monopoly of court officials. One who searches for wisdom can know the order that underlies all creation and can make his or her choices accordingly. At its roots the oldest part of the Hebrew wisdom tradition is very close to the Deuteronomic tradition, in which virtue is always promptly rewarded and sin is always thoroughly punished.

But is it true that all suffering is a punishment for one's own sins? The author of the Book of Job is willing to accept what Job's three friends cannot: the innocent often suffer. Yet neither Job nor his friends are ready to say that there is a life beyond this one, a life in which the apparently prosperous sinner will be punished and the innocent sufferer will be rewarded—in short, a life where the order of God's universe will prevail forever.

At the end of the book Job is confident that God has taken his side, but he is not specific about when and how. Belief in a life beyond this one, where God's values will be vindicated, began in Judaism only around the third century B.C. At the time of Jesus the Pharisees believed in an afterlife for each person, but many Jews did not.

The remainder of this chapter will explore images of God in three wisdom writings (Proverbs, Sirach, and Wisdom) in the order of their final composition.

Proverbs: A God Ready to Share Wisdom With Humans

The Book of Proverbs begins with a prologue, followed by two collections attributed to Solomon, sayings of other wise men, collections credited to non-Hebrew sages, a series of numerical proverbs, and a poem about the ideal wife. The sections identified with Solomon are probably contemporary with him or were written shortly after his death. Typical examples:

> Yahweh does not let the upright go hungry,
>   but he thwarts the greed of the wicked (Prv 10:3).
> The fear of Yahweh is a school of wisdom,
>   before there can be glory, there must be humility (Prv 15:33).

According to the editors of the *New Jerusalem Bible*,

> In the two primitive collections, the dominant tone is that of human, worldly wisdom, disconcerting to the Christian reader, though even here one proverb in every seven is religious in theme. This religious teaching is not speculative but practical: God rewards truth, charity, purity of heart, humility, and punishes their contrary vices.[11]

Those tempted to dismiss many of the proverbs as secular should remember that in the ancient world religion influenced all of life because all life comes from God. Thus a strict division of sacred and secular is both impossible and undesirable. The Book of Proverbs emphasizes the importance and religious significance of simple pleasures such as a well-ordered household, a respectful family, and proper social relationships.

Throughout Hebrew wisdom literature, the fool is not so much a person who lacks intelligence as one who has no sense of God or appreciation of the Law. Failing to recognize the order God has placed in creation, the fool thinks creation can be completely shaped according to his or her own purposes.

Wisdom prepares a banquet and invites all to eat her bread and drink her wine, leaving foolishness behind. Folly, however, has her own banquet and sits at her door, inviting those who pass by. Each person will eat at one banquet or the other and reap the consequences.

In the Book of Proverbs God is often like an anxious father wanting to impart wisdom but knowing that this is impossible without cooperation from the intended recipient. Although fear of Yahweh is praised as the beginning of wisdom, this fear does not paralyze but rather energizes, for it gives the person prudence in knowing what he or she should do and courage to act honestly and consistently.

Those who think of the God of the Hebrew scriptures as harsh and aloof probably have not read the Book of Proverbs, especially the prologue, which explains God's efforts to make wisdom available to those willing to seek it and reorder their lives accordingly. The Lord of all creation certainly cannot pour wisdom into the foolish, self-sufficient person but can only offer wisdom to everyone who will accept a reverential fear of God and the resulting discipline of life.

Sirach: A God Whose Law Brings Wisdom

Around 180 B.C. the Jerusalem-based scribe Sirach saw Jews compromising their national and religious identity by accepting Greek customs. The Syrians, who controlled the land of Judah at that time, were promoting "Hellenization," adaptation of Greek culture to local cultures and thus the creation of a common culture. Hellenization meant not only learning Greek and wearing Greek-style clothing, but also exchanging belief in one God for polytheism. Jews who accepted that exchange were committing corporate suicide, religiously speaking. While the rewards for uncritically accepting Hellenization increased, so did the penalties for not becoming assimilated into the general population.

Stung by the suggestion that the Hellenistic world has a monopoly on wisdom, Sirach writes a book to show that true wisdom is found in Judaism, especially in observing the Law of Moses and carrying out the Temple worship. Sirach writes not only for those in Palestine but also for Jews in Egypt and elsewhere in the Diaspora; his grandson will translate the book into Greek. The conflict over Hellenization represents the background for the Maccabean revolt (168–160 B.C.), which brings freedom from Syria but an alliance with and eventual subjugation to the Roman Empire.

Jews and most Protestants consider the Book of Sirach apocryphal; the Hebrew canon of the Old Testament does not include it. Catholics and Orthodox Christians call Sirach deutero-canonical because the Greek canon of the Old Testament does include the book.

According to Sirach all wisdom comes from the Lord who alone is truly wise, who pours out wisdom on those who love her. Fear of the Lord is wisdom's basis; those who keep the Lord's commandments will receive this priceless gift. People who are being tested should trust in the Lord and remain faithful. Those who are wise respect their aging parents, are charitable to the poor, and ready to repent of their sins. Sirach advises them:

> Be steady in your convictions,
>   and be a person of your word.
> Be quick to listen,
>   and deliberate in giving an answer (Sir 5:10–11).

After giving advice on raising children, dealing with quick-tempered people, avoiding envy, and many other everyday topics, Sirach urges trust in the Lord. Although Sirach does not believe in an afterlife, he says that the sinner will not profit from his sins and the patience of the devout will be rewarded. However, he does not explain when and how that takes place.

When Wisdom herself speaks, she reveals her divine origin. When she sought a place to rest, God instructed her to pitch her tent in Jacob and make Israel her inheritance. Thus she settled there and prospered, inviting all to taste her fruits.

> They who eat me will hunger for more,
>   they who drink me will thirst for more.
> No one who obeys me will ever have to blush,
>   no one who acts as I dictate will ever sin (Sir 24:21–22).

After almost twenty more chapters of advice, Sirach begins to praise God's glory seen in nature and in human history. Sirach praises pious men loyal to God, observant of the Law, and blessed in their descendants.

> Their bodies have been buried in peace,
>   and their name lives on for all generations.
> The peoples will proclaim their wisdom,
>   the assembly will celebrate their praises (Sir 44:14–15).

Among the kings, Sirach praises only David, Hezekiah, and Josiah.

Sirach presents a God who excels the wisdom of the Greeks, a God who long ago brought wisdom to the Jews through the Law of Moses and the Temple worship. The Lord of history mentioned by other prophets, such as Second and Third Isaiah, comes to full stature in Sirach's sweeping review of human history. God's wisdom, however, also touches everyday concerns like raising children, controlling one's tongue, giving alms, and not being mastered by wine.

Wisdom: A God Who Protects Lovers of Wisdom

In the city of Alexandria during the first century before Christ, a Jewish sage meditated on the Law, the prophets, and the previous wisdom writings; he was troubled that some Jews felt they had to follow Greek ideas and customs to arrive at true wisdom. This sage was annoyed by the suggestion that the relative insignificance of Jews in a world governed by pagans was proof that Israel's faith was somehow deficient. In addition, he felt that the problem of innocent suffering (already treated in Job, Qoheleth, and several psalms) cried out for a more satisfying answer.

The author of the Book of Wisdom is both traditional and innovative. He is traditional because he has meditated long and hard on the Hebrew scriptures and because he presents this book as Solomon's instruction to help other kings attain wisdom. He describes the providence of God at work in Jewish history, especially in the Exodus. However, this writer is not afraid to innovate. He links Wisdom to the Spirit of the Lord and shows Wisdom teaching the cardinal virtues honored by Greek philosophers—prudence, fortitude, justice, and temperance. The break with tradition comes in the author's daring response to the problem of innocent suffering:

There is a life beyond this one where those who have loved God's wisdom and staked their lives on it will live happily with God; those who have rejected God's wisdom will be bitterly separated from God. Although other scriptural authors try to take us inside the reasoning process of sinners,[12] this author may have succeeded best of all.

The godless, he says, consider Death their friend and wear themselves out for him. Since they believe their life is short, they must, therefore, leave signs of their revelry everywhere. To the godless the upright man is a constant annoyance, for "his kind of life is not like other people's, / and his ways are quite different" (Wis 2:15). They decide that "if the upright man is God's son" (Wis 2:18), God will rescue him. The Jewish sage here describes the accusation made against his people by Gentiles and Jews who have been totally Hellenized. The godless are blind to God's plan for creation; they do not see that God made humans in his own image and intended them to be immortal. Death came into the world through the devil's envy.

> But the souls of the upright are in the hands of
>   God,
> and no torment can touch them.
> To the unenlightened, they appeared to die,
> their departure was regarded as a disaster,
> their leaving us like an annihilation;
> but they are at peace.
> If, as it seemed to us, they suffered punishment,
> their hope was rich with immortality,
> slight was their correction, great will their bless-
>   ings be.
> God was putting them to the test
> and has proved them worthy to be with him (Wis
>   3:1–5).

Men and women who have scorned wisdom and discipline will be wretched; when they are called to judgment, they will see the folly of their lives.

Chapters 6–9 portray Solomon instructing gentile
kings about the divine origins of all authority and the
need to pursue wisdom in order to rule well. Though
Solomon appears to be addressing kings, he stresses
that he is mortal like everyone else. Perhaps the Jewish
sage is using Solomon to suggest that wisdom is within
the grasp of each person—king or commoner. Solomon
prays that Wisdom will teach him what is pleasing to
God and enable him to govern justly. With Wisdom's
help, Solomon can comprehend the will of God.

Next the Jewish sage traces the role of Wisdom
in history, paying special attention to Wisdom's role in
leading the Chosen People from the corruption of Egypt
in the Exodus.

In the Book of Wisdom we meet a God whose justice extends to a life beyond this one, a life where the
godless are punished and the wise receive the reward
of a life based on God's wisdom and sovereignty over
all creation. Wisdom, once considered the monopoly of
kings and court officials, has now been offered to all
those ready to esteem it more valuable than gold or silver. This last book of the Hebrew scriptures in order of
composition portrays a God whom some of the earlier
writers might not have readily recognized, but nonetheless a God revealing tremendous love and providence
for Israel and the rest of the human family.

A Word of Caution

I hope that this chapter has given you some indi-
cation of the many images of God in the Hebrew scriptures. By describing these writings in roughly chronological order of final composition, I do not intend to suggest
that newer images of God make older ones obsolete. But

I think we should know that a simple phrase like *God's will* means one thing in the Book of Joshua (conquering Canaan) and something else in the Book of Wisdom (pursuing Wisdom and living accordingly). The God concerned with the fidelity of tribes and families to his Law (Deuteronomy) is concerned for the fidelity of individuals even apart from their relatives (Ezekiel). The God of thunder and lightning at Mount Sinai (Exodus) is likewise a loving spouse (Hosea), a compassionate shepherd (Ezekiel), and the one who guarantees the immortality of each person (Wisdom).

I have asked readers to spend time and energy on the images of God in the Hebrew scriptures because I firmly believe that sweeping generalizations regarding this material have caused Christians problems with their images of God.

For Personal Reflection

1. Do I feel more comfortable with one of the literary/theological traditions in the Pentateuch? Can I see its possible limitations and the usefulness of other theological traditions?
2. Do I find some stories in the Hebrew scriptures an obstacle to faith? Have I prayed and studied these stories?
3. In what way is God a jealous God? In what way is that image of God inadequate?
4. Has smugness about God ever made me blind to my own sins? Is that still happening in some corner of my life?
5. What does God mean in saying, "Faithful love is what pleases me, not sacrifice; knowledge of God, not burnt offerings" (Hos 6:6)?
6. Is there some sense in which God is trying to breathe new life into the dry bones of my life? Am I fighting that new life in some way?

For Group Discussion

1. Are the Hebrew scriptures mostly *terra incognita* for us? If
   so, does that affect our ability to understand and appreciate
   the New Testament? What can we do about that?
2. Is applying human characteristics to God always a bad
   practice? a good practice? How can we tell when our language about God has reached the end of its usefulness and
   threatens to distort God?
3. Do you consider anyone living today a prophet? Who?
   Why?
4. Do many people think of God as parent (father or mother)
   as presented in Hosea, chapter 11? Is that image any more
   or less "the God of the Old Testament" than God on Mount
   Sinai with thunder and smoke?
5. In what sense is God's wisdom mundane, concerned with
   matters we might not even consider religious?

Further Resources

The Bible Today, a periodical published by Liturgical Press (Col-
   legeville, MN) presents solid, popular articles on the He-
   brew scriptures and the New Testament.
Lawrence Boadt, *Reading the Old Testament*, rev. ed. (Mahwah,
   NJ: Paulist Press, 1988).
Dermot Cox, *Man's Anger and God's Silence: The Book of Job*
   (Mahwah, NJ: Paulist Press, 1989).
Anthony Gilles, *People of the Book* (Cincinnati, OH: St. Anthony
   Messenger Press, 1983).
Abraham Heschel, *Prophets* (New York: Harper and Row,
   1971).
Conrad L'Heureux, *Life Journey and the Old Testament: An Ex-
   periential Approach to the Bible and Personal Transformation*
   (Mahwah, NJ: Paulist Press, 1986).
John L. McKenzie, *Dictionary of the Bible* (New York: Mac-
   millan, 1967). This illustrated, 954-page book explains
   people, places and key concepts of the Bible.
New American Bible (Catholic Publishers, Inc.) various editions.
   One recent edition moves in the direction of using inclu-
   sive language for the New Testament. The *NAB* text is

used for the liturgy in most Roman Catholic churches. Good notes.

Renee Rust, *Making the Psalms Your Prayer: Insights, Exercises, Resources* (Cincinnati, OH: St. Anthony Messenger Press, 1987). This book's appendix A2 lists twenty-three images of God used in the psalms.

Vawter, Bruce, C.M., *Job and Jonah: Questioning the Hidden God* (Mahwah, NJ: Paulist Press, 1983).

THREE

Images of God in the New Testament

Because the Hebrew scriptures were finalized in a one thousand-year period and the New Testament writings were completed in approximately seventy years, between A.D. 50 and 120, we might expect much more uniformity in the New Testament images of God. In fact, however, the variations are quite surprising. The New Testament authors came from diverse backgrounds and addressed churches geographically and sometimes culturally distant from one another, churches facing distinct challenges to their faith.

This chapter focuses on images of God in First Corinthians, James, Luke, and Matthew.[1] This choice allows for several connections with the previous chapter, plus images not found in the Hebrew scriptures. Although these New Testament writings will be considered in their probable order of final composition, this does not imply that later writers knew all earlier writings that were eventually accepted into the canon.

First Corinthians and James concern specific moral and doctrinal problems; Paul and James, however, intend as well to correct certain ideas and practices based on incomplete or twisted images of God. For example, First Corinthians deals with a eucharist intended to praise God but which, in fact, fosters division within the community. The gospels are problem-oriented in many respects, but they too tend to set forth certain images of God the community needs to remember, value, and imitate.

First Corinthians: An Image of
One God, One Lord, Many Gifts

In A.D. 50–52, Paul spent eighteen months preaching in Corinth, first to Jews in the synagogue, and after he was expelled from the synagogue, to the Gentiles. First Corinthians dates from A.D. 57 and is probably the oldest New Testament writing after First and Second Thessalonians. In First Corinthians, Paul gives doctrinal and moral teaching on subjects that are causing divisions within the church in Corinth.

According to Paul, the Christian community in Corinth lacks no divine gift as it waits for our Lord Jesus Christ to be revealed. Gifted as they were, however, factions had developed.

Paul has preached a crucified Christ, but since many Jews in Corinth are looking for "signs" and Gentiles are seeking "wisdom," Paul responds:

> We are preaching a crucified Christ: to the Jews an obstacle they cannot get over, to the gentiles foolishness, but to those who have been called, whether they are Jews or Greeks, a Christ who is both the power of God and the wisdom of God. God's folly is wiser than human wisdom, and God's weakness is stronger than human strength (1 Cor 1:23–25).

The authors of the earliest wisdom writings in the Hebrew scriptures could not have imagined a crucified savior as God's wisdom, but the author of the Suffering Servant songs in Second Isaiah might have had an easier time.

Paul has come to the Corinthians not as a persuasive orator or a convincing philosopher but as one who speaks in terms learned from the Spirit. The apostles work hard as God's servants, but only God gives the growth. The Christians in Corinth are God's farm, God's building, a temple of God in which the Spirit of God lives. Rather than fight about their gifts and their position within the community, they should remember that they belong to Christ, who belongs to God.

Although some people had thought that God would protect the apostles from all danger, Paul counters that the apostles are weak, disgraced, homeless, cursed, and insulted. A God with messengers such as these must be revealing something about himself, about his decision to respect human freedom even when it is used against his apostles.

When Paul cautions the Corinthians against sexual immorality—the city had a reputation for this—he uses the image of the individual as a temple of the Holy Spirit. The Corinthians have been bought at a great price and so must use their bodies for the glory of God. Although pagan gods might be content with prescribed sacrifices and observance of a few special days, every aspect of life is important to the God whom Paul preaches, every day is a moment to grow toward God or away from him.

Everyone, says Paul, needs to guard against taking God for granted, as some of the Hebrews did during the Exodus. Whatever trials the Corinthians endure are not beyond their ability to withstand.

You can trust that God will not let you be put to the test beyond your strength, but with any trial will also provide a way out by enabling you to put up with it (1 Cor 10:13).

Paul, a veteran apostle, knows God's tolerance of evil and the divine resolve that it will not prevail.

Perhaps no other problem within the Christian community in Corinth illustrates their varying images of God as the way they celebrate the eucharist. A common meal precedes the eucharist, but the meal is common only in the sense that small groups of friends share food and drink with one another (to the point that some were drunk by the time the eucharist starts), while others go hungry. What should build up the community is threatening to tear it down. Paul recalls the tradition he has received and handed on about the eucharist—how Jesus intends that it should proclaim his death until he comes. Those who participate in the eucharist without recognizing the body of the Lord (the transformed bread and wine, and also the community gathered in his name) are eating and drinking their own condemnation.

Although the Corinthians may have been the first Christians to introduce social and economic divisions into the eucharist, they were hardly the last. And whenever their mistake is repeated, a distorted image of God is being presented as genuine. Earlier the prophet Amos had criticized religious celebrations that people left only to return immediately to using dishonest weights in the market. And the prophet Isaiah had predicted a banquet where rich and poor would be equally welcome.

The factions present during the eucharist at Corinth may be related to the disputes over the gifts of the Spirit and their relative importance before God. Paul explains:

> There are many gifts, but it is always the same Spirit; there are many different ways of serving, but it is always the same Lord. There are many different forms of activity, but in everybody it is the same God who is at work in them all. The particular manifestation of the Spirit granted

to each one is to be used for the general good
(1 Cor 12:4–7).

Any idea of a monopoly on the charisms needed in the
church is a subtle form of idolatry, an attempt to make
God into one's own image.

I think that Paul brings into focus varying images
of God when he writes:

> Love is always patient and kind; love is never
> jealous; love is not boastful or conceited, it is
> never rude and never seeks its own advantage,
> it does not take offense or store up grievances.
> Love does not rejoice at wrongdoing, but finds
> its joy in the truth. It is always ready to make
> allowances, to trust, to hope and to endure what-
> ever comes (1 Cor 13:4–7).

When Paul describes love, isn't he also describing God,
presenting a series of related images of God?

Even when Christians deal with difficult cases—for
example, Paul told the Corinthians to expel the inces-
tuous man from their assembly to impress on him the
seriousness of his sin—they should act with love. If they
fail to do so, they will inevitably use their gifts to call attention to the gift, weakening the community for which
the gift is intended.

First Corinthians presents several images—the crucified savior as the power and the wisdom of God, God
as the one who makes the plant grow, God as one who
raises perishable bodies to an imperishable life—to help
the Corinthian Christians grow toward a more mature
faith and more selfless service to one another.

James: A God for Rich and Poor Alike

The Letter of James presents God as a just judge
who hears the cries of the oppressed; God scorns the
idea that he is indebted to the rich and rejects the poor.

The entire letter is a written sermon on moral issues, especially the treatment of the poor. In this letter we meet the God of the Beatitudes, the God who sustains persecuted believers, the God described in the Hebrew wisdom writings, and the God who expects faith to issue forth in good deeds.

The recipients of the letter were Jewish Christians living outside Palestine, probably before the destruction of Jerusalem in A.D. 70. The writer is James, "servant of God and of the Lord Jesus Christ" (v.1), probably not James the Greater (son of Zebedee) or James the Lesser (son of Alphaeus), but rather James "the brother of the Lord" (cf. Mt 13:55) and head of the church in Jerusalem until his martyrdom in A.D. 62. Some exegetes suggest that this letter claims the authority of that well-known Christian leader, but actually dates from a later period. In any case, the letter is inspired, and the writer is a "Judaeo-Christian sage who has rethought the maxims of the Jewish Wisdom tradition in the Light of his Master's teachings and is able to re-present them in an original way."[2]

Faithful to the later wisdom writings, which often spoke of a faith tested by affliction (see Sir 2:5), James says:

> My brothers, consider it a great joy when trials of many kinds come upon you, for you well know that the testing of your faith produces perseverance, and perseverance must complete its work so that you will become fully developed, complete, not deficient in any way (Jas 1:2–4).

Those who lack wisdom should seek it from God "who gives to all generously and without scolding" (Jas 1:5). Those who are being tempted should not say that God is tempting them or is putting them to the test:

Everyone is put to the test by being attracted and seduced by that person's own wrong desire. Then the desire conceives and gives birth to sin, and when sin reaches full growth, it gives birth to death (Jas 1:14–15).

Perhaps some recipients of this letter thought their anger reflected God's. After advising them to be quick to listen but slow to speak and to become angry, James adds, "God's saving justice is never served by human anger; so do away with all impurities and remnants of evil. Humbly welcome the Word which has been planted in you and can save your souls" (Jas 1:20–21).

Later he adds, "Pure, unspoilt religion, in the eyes of God our Father, is this: coming to the help of orphans and widows in their hardships, and keeping oneself uncontaminated by the world" (Jas 1:27). The author criticized any Christian whose only response to naked and hungry people would be wishing them well. James recalls again the connection between images of God, oneself, and others. Apparently James was worried that not everyone understood this connection and that some people worshipped a God they thought despised the poor as much as they did.

Against a faith that presents itself as an inner feeling or idea but does not result in concrete action, James says: "How does it help, my brothers, when someone who has never done a single good act claims to have faith?" (Jas 2:14). James recalls Abraham's readiness to sacrifice Isaac as an example of a faith in action, a faith that is rich in good deeds.

After admonitions about controlling one's tongue and the need to avoid jealousy and selfish ambition, James describes "love of the world" as "hatred for God" (Jas 4:4). "World" here means everything that is opposed to God, not God's creation and the place where our faith must be lived out. He warns the rich not to be over-confident of their wealth or the amount of time they have for using it.

> Well now, you rich! Lament, weep for the miseries that are coming to you. Your wealth is rotting, your clothes are all moth-eaten. All your gold and your silver are corroding away, and the same corrosion will be a witness against you and eat into your body. It is like a fire which you have stored up for the final days. Can you hear crying out against you the wages which you kept back from the laborers mowing your fields? The cries of the reapers have reached the ears of the Lord Sabaoth. On earth you have had a life of comfort and luxury; in the time of slaughter you went on eating to your heart's content. It was you who condemned the upright and killed them; they offered you no resistance (Jas 5:1–6).

The people warned by this passage have interwoven mistaken images of God, themselves, and others; only if those images are straightened out, correctly related to one another, and then acted upon can the punishment foretold be avoided.

The Letter of James does not explain every aspect of Christian faith—only those matters of greatest urgency for the community for which it was written. However, no other New Testament writing is so emphatic about the connection between faith and good deeds and about the blasphemy inherent in the idea that God automatically loves the rich and despises the poor.

Luke: A God of Forgiveness and Upholder of the Poor

Luke writes his gospel for gentile Christians, who need to see that the message of Jesus is for them as well as for the Jews. The gospel of Luke and the Acts of the Apostles, also by Luke, show that Jesus' work is being continued by his church and that the good news is going out to all peoples, to every corner of the earth. The Spirit guides the church as it continues the mission of Jesus. Luke shows Christianity, not as a political movement or a sect open to a select few, but as a religion open to all those ready to become disciples of Jesus. Luke emphasizes not a quick return of the Lord but rather how the story of Jesus fits into current world events.

Luke explains that this ordered account of Jesus' life and ministry is intended to help Theophilus "learn how well founded the teaching is that you have received" (Lk 1:4). Theophilus may be a historical person or a literary device to identify a gentile audience.

Luke opens his account by interweaving the announcements of the birth of John the Baptist and Jesus, their birth and circumcision, and their hidden life before their public ministry. Throughout the infancy narrative we meet faithful men and women, attentive to the Lord in prayer and ready to carry out what he asks of them: Zechariah and Elizabeth, Mary and Joseph, Simeon and Anna. These three couples are *anawim*, poor in material goods but rich in the faith that God will carry out what he has promised.[3] These prayerful women and men praise God's steadfast love (Mary's *Magnificat* and Zechariah's *Benedictus*) and revelation to Israel and to the nations (Simeon's *Nunc Dimittis*). Their images of God might have seemed unsophisticated to those well-versed in the Law, but those images were both traditional and open to prayerful reflection and development. The Judean people who heard of John's birth and Zechariah's prayer "treasured it in their hearts" (Lk 1:66); Mary, too, treasured what she had seen and pondered these things in her heart.

John the Baptist preaches repentance for the forgiveness of sins and calls his followers to be baptized.

Since their repentance must bear fruit in changed lives, they cannot simply congratulate themselves on being children of Abraham. Those who ask what they must do receive answers tailored to their life situation (the rich, tax collectors, soldiers). Repentance includes changed images of God, oneself, and others and has very practical, immediate consequences.

Differing images of God are at work in one of the best-known New Testament parables, which is found only in the gospel of Luke: the parable of the good Samaritan. The introduction to the parable is crucial, for here a lawyer asks Jesus what he must do to inherit eternal life. When Jesus asks what the Law says, the man responds, *"You must love the Lord your God with all your heart, with all your soul, with all your strength, and with all your mind, and your neighbor as yourself"* (Lk 10:27). Jesus affirms this answer and tells the man to follow it. But the man responds by asking, "And who is my neighbor?" (Lk 10:29).

Jesus tells a story rich in ambiguity: a man travelling in open country (no man's land, so to speak), beaten, robbed, and left half-dead; a priest and Levite, who pass on the other side of the road; a Samaritan, who is already in hostile territory but who bandages the man, takes him to an inn, and leaves himself open for future medical costs. Then Jesus asks the lawyer who was neighbor to the man left half-dead. The lawyer responds, "The one who showed pity towards him." "Go, and do the same yourself" (Lk 10:37), says Jesus finishing the story.

The lawyer seemed to have a problem with defining *neighbor*; that difficulty undoubtedly affected his ability to love God with all his heart, soul, strength, and mind. If he hoped for a more restrictive definition of neighbor, how likely was he to love God with an ever-expanding love? The lawyer was probably tempted to love only a tidy God and a very well-defined neighbor, but perhaps he accepted the challenge posed by Jesus. Certainly this parable praises an ever-expanding love of God and neighbor—even when the situation is ambiguous and the risks are great.

Chapter 15 contains two parables unique to Luke's gospel. Again the context is crucial for understanding the evangelist's purpose: "The tax collectors and sinners, however, were all crowding round to listen to him, and the Pharisees and scribes complained saying, 'This man welcomes sinners and eats with them'" (Lk 15:1).

The story of the shepherd leaving the ninety-nine sheep to search for the lost one is also told in Matthew, but in Luke's version Jesus adds, "In the same way, I tell you, there will be more rejoicing in heaven over one sinner repenting than over ninety-nine upright people who have no need of repentance" (Lk 15:7). The story of the woman who rejoices on finding a lost coin makes the same point and prepares for perhaps the most famous parable in the New Testament: the Prodigal Son.

Since the younger son is bored by working on the father's estate, he demands and receives his inheritance early. Once he spends all his money and is reduced to feeding pigs though hungry himself, the younger son comes to his senses (repents) and decides he would be better off as a worker on his father's farm than in his present condition.

The father, however, will not hear of such an arrangement. This son who was "dead" has come to life again, and that calls for a feast. Enter the dutiful but self-righteous older son, offended by his father's generosity. His accusations about his brother are true (the inheritance *was* squandered on riotous living), but how could the elder son be so sure? And why does he refer to "this son of yours" rather than say "my brother"? Whereas the younger son had once seen his father as a hindrance to "the good life" and is now satisfied simply not to starve, the elder brother loves his father but sees him as a partner in a contract that must be honored—even if that means no feast for the return of the prodigal.

Who, then, is the prodigal? In an obvious sense, the younger brother. But in a subtle and no less real way, the elder brother is also prodigal. Though he shows stinginess in begrudging his brother a feast, the older brother is prodigal in squandering his faithful service by using it to justify a bottomless self-pity. And the father's love toward both sons is obviously prodigal.

The younger brother's return produces a marvelous irony: the one who was dead has come back to life, but we realize that the one who had seemed very much alive is, in fact, dead (unable to share the joy of repentance). Perhaps the elder brother eventually came to his senses, but Jesus leaves the story unfinished in order to emphasize his point about the joy in heaven over the conversion of a single person.

This multifaceted story could also be called the parable of a father's generous love or the parable of the self-righteous older brother. The latter title would emphasize the context in which Jesus tells the parable— scribes and Pharisees complaining about sinners and tax collectors.

The story of the rich man and Lazarus, also unique to Luke, presents a God who is kind, merciful, and ready to forgive while the person lives. At the same time it shows a God unwilling to trivialize a life of selfishness by forgiving someone who repents after he has died. Nor is this God ready to send people back from the dead as a warning to others. Speaking in God's name Abraham says that they should listen to Moses and the prophets. Lazarus and the rich man differ in many obvious respects, and perhaps in a less obvious way. They do not have the same images of God, and that is reflected in the way they treat other people. Eventually their images of God, self, and other people reinforce one another—for better or for worse.

When Zacchaeus the tax collector repents, he accepts a larger and more generous image of God, which has very definite, immediate consequences for the way Zacchaeus treats others. He starts with restitution, and we suspect he is moving toward the Good Samaritan's kind of dangerous, open-ended love in an ambiguous situation. Ironically, Zacchaeus changes his image of God and neighbor, but many other people refuse to change their image of Zacchaeus. We can hope they were more open to accepting a wider image of God than they already had, but the evangelist deliberately leaves that as an open question.

Luke's account of the passion and death of Jesus is full of people whose images of God are in flux: Judas, Peter, Pilate, Herod, the good thief, and the centurion at the crucifixion. Judas, Pilate, and Herod apparently finally chose an image of God that would not threaten their mindset; after his initial denials, Peter grew in faith, changing his life to harmonize with his more truthful image of God.

Only Luke presents the story of Jesus accompanying the two disciples on the road to Emmaus. When Jesus meets these disciples, they are trying to sort out what has happened in the past three days. Their ideas of God are likewise in flux. They tell Jesus, "Our own hope had been that he would be the one to set Israel free" (Lk 24:21). Although the conversation on the road to Emmaus is about what kind of messiah God would send, in fact the disciples are also discussing their

images of God, the kind who would—or would not—
send a messiah who could be crucified.

Jesus explains to these two disciples why it was
necessary that the Christ should suffer before entering
his glory. Jesus then cites the scriptures to explain the
passages that refer to him. What is he doing here? Isn't
he helping these two disciples to readjust their images
of God, to deepen those images? When the disciples in-
vite Jesus to stay with them for supper, they suddenly
recognize him in the breaking of the bread and ask one
another, "Did not our hearts burn within us as he talked
to us on the road and explained the scriptures to us?"
(Lk 24:32).

The encounter with Jesus has been a moment of
conversion for them, a moment in which they could
recognize him as he is, free from their customary standards of success and failure. Immediately they rush off
to Jerusalem to tell the apostles what they have experienced. As they are speaking, Jesus appears again. To
assure them he is no ghost, he eats a piece of grilled
fish. Then he reminds them of his prediction that everything written about him in the scriptures had to be
fulfilled.

> "So it is written that the Christ would suffer and
> on the third day rise from the dead, and that,
> in his name, repentance for the forgiveness of
> sins would be preached to all nations, beginning
> from Jerusalem. You are witnesses to this" (Lk
> 24:46–47).

If Jesus helped them to understand the scriptures better,
he must have pointed out some of their misconceptions
about God. Jesus did not change the scriptures they
already knew but rather showed how they had misunderstood what was there, probably by making God
too much like themselves, a God who operated by their

rules of logic, which certainly did not include a crucified savior. Only because they were willing to grow in
their images of God and to receive the Holy Spirit's assistance for further growth, could these disciples be the
witnesses whom Jesus needed.

Luke presents a God faithful to his promises, a God
who seeks out the powerless and rejected (sick, women,
tax collectors) and invites them to become disciples, a
God who does not want people to interpret wealth as an
automatic sign of divine favor, a God whose Holy Spirit
will continue to guide the disciples. Luke describes a
savior ready to suffer and die for the sins of the world,
a Jesus anxious to walk with disciples (to Emmaus and
elsewhere), helping them correct their misunderstandings of the scriptures and strengthening them to proclaim the good news.

Matthew: A God Whose Kingdom
Is Imminent and Universal

The gospel of Matthew was written for Christians
who had close ties to Judaism and needed to see how
Jesus Christ both developed and went beyond the Mosaic Law. They needed to understand the continuity of
their faith with that of Israel, as well as the uniqueness
of Jesus and his invitation to a different standard of values. The author is certainly familiar with the rabbinic
teaching style and may even have been a former rabbi.
He seeks to help Christians uneasy with a faith in which
the Law of Moses does not play the dominant role. Jesus the Messiah fills the vacuum created by the Law's
decreasing importance.

Matthew's gospel frequently quotes the Hebrew
scriptures or makes allusions to them. As in the Pentateuch's Elohist tradition, God frequently communicates
through dreams. Joseph has three (do not hesitate to
take Mary as your wife, flee into Egypt, and return now

to your homeland). The Magi are likewise warned in a dream. Indeed, they show that all nations have come to honor Jesus—much as Isaiah prophesied that all nations would come to Jerusalem to worship God there.

Matthew's gospel resembles the Book of Deuteronomy more than it resembles any other book in the Hebrew scriptures. Deuteronomy contains five great discourses by Moses on keeping the Law and remaining holy to the Lord. The Sermon on the Mount (Mt 5:1–7:29) is the first of Jesus' five discourses to promote respect for the Mosaic Law, but the Sermon on the Mount also points out the need to see Jesus as superior to the Law and as its best interpreter. Jesus comes not to abolish the Law but to bring it to completion (Mt 5:17).

In doing so Jesus must challenge the Pharisees, who favor the system of oral tradition. In this, the Pharisees made an important contribution to Judaism by legitimating a dynamic element. However, they sometimes allowed oral tradition to become very restrictive, even nullifying divine commands. Jesus honors the Law but calls for a sense of personal discretion and responsibility. The Sadducees, on the other hand, accepted only what God revealed in the Pentateuch as inspired; thus the Sadducees would not accept a life beyond this one because that belief became clear to some Jews only 200 years before Christ's birth.

Jesus tells his disciples that their uprightness must surpass that of the scribes and Pharisees. Six times in Matthew 5:20–48 Jesus says "You have heard how it was said . . . [not to kill, commit adultery, divorce, break an oath, eye for an eye, love your neighbor, and hate your enemy] but I say to you," and then Jesus presents a more open-ended, more demanding moral standard (seeking reconciliation before offering sacrifice, not looking at a woman lustfully, and so on). Jesus says that if the disciples love only those who love them, they are no better than the tax collectors, who do the same. If they save their greetings for their brothers, they have not surpassed the Gentiles, who do the same. Jesus concludes, "You must therefore set no bounds to your love, just as your heavenly Father sets none to his" (Mt 5:48).

The evangelist makes several references to the Hebrew scriptures. When Jesus cures the sick and those possessed by evil spirits, Matthew adds: "This was to fulfill what was spoken by the prophet Isaiah: *He himself bore our sicknesses away and carried our diseases*" (Mt 8:17). When the Pharisees complain that Jesus eats with sinners, Jesus responds that the sick need a doctor, not the healthy. Then he adds, "Go and learn the meaning of the words: *Mercy is what pleases me, not sacrifice* [Hos 6:6]" (Mt 9:13). The same verse is quoted again in Matthew 12:7 when the Pharisees complain that the disciples are breaking the sabbath law by picking ears of corn and eating them on the sabbath.

Jesus feels sorry for the crowds as he travels through villages, teaching and curing: "They were harassed and dejected, like sheep without a shepherd" (Mt 9:36).[4]

Jesus warns those he cures not to make him known. Matthew then adds, "This was to fulfill what was spoken by the prophet Isaiah: *Look! My servant whom I have chosen, my beloved, in whom my soul delights*" (Mt 12:16–18). When some scribes and Pharisees ask for a sign, Jesus responds that they will receive only the sign of Jonah: The Son of Man will be in the heart of the earth three days and three nights. That image is further developed when Jesus reminds his listeners that the pagan Ninevites converted when Jonah preached, but they have not.

When Jesus describes the kingdom of Heaven by means of parables (sower and the seed, weeds among the wheat, mustard seed, yeast, hidden treasure, pearl of great price, and the dragnet), he asks the people if they have understood these. When they say they do, he adds: "Well then, every scribe who becomes a disciple of the kingdom of Heaven is like a householder who brings out from his storeroom new things as well as old" (Mt 13:52). With this verse Matthew may be drawing a self-portrait, since the scribe who becomes a disciple of Jesus has access to the teachings of Jesus as well as to the Hebrew scriptures.

When the disciples are accused of not observing the traditions of the elders (not washing their hands), Jesus criticizes the scribes and Pharisees for using these traditions to make God's word ineffective; he shows how they have nullified the command to love one's parents.

To whom was Jesus directing the parable of the one son who said he would not work in his father's vineyard but did so and of the other son who agreed to work there but did not? Jesus was speaking to the chief priests and elders of the people, and when he asked them which son did the father's will, they indicated the first son. Jesus responded:

> "In truth I tell you, tax collectors and prostitutes are making their way into the kingdom of God before you. For John [the Baptist] came to you, showing the way of uprightness, but you did not believe him, and yet the tax collectors and pros-titutes did. Even after seeing that, you refused to think better of it and believe in him" (Mt 21:31–32).

It seems to me that here Jesus challenges images of God that have become too cozy, too domesticated. Wasn't it for statements such as these that Jesus was eventually accused of blasphemy? In his famous parable about the last judgment, Jesus says that those saved have fed him when he was hungry, clothed him when he was naked, and so on. When those condemned to eternal punishment ask when they failed to respond to Jesus' hunger and thirst, loneliness as a stranger, and so on, he answers, "In so far as you neglected to do this to one of the least of these, you neglected to do it to me" (Mt 25:45). The parable is very familiar, but how often do we realize that the difference between the saved and the condemned lies in their images of God and how they acted on those images? Our images of God undergird our most simple acts of charity or refusals of charity.

As Jesus hangs on the cross, passers-by urge him to save himself if he is God's son and come down from the cross. They are not prepared to believe in a crucified savior. The chief priests, scribes, and elders repeat this taunt, saying that they will believe in Jesus as king of Israel if he immediately comes down from the cross. Perhaps those who taunted Jesus on the cross did so because that was their only way of answering his challenge to their smug, self-serving images of God.

Matthew has the challenge of describing a God who stands by his revelation in the Law and the prophets while presenting a kingdom of Heaven unknown to previous generations. In the gospel of Matthew we meet a God who must be recognized in the hungry, the homeless, and the naked. According to the evangelist, God uses the church to continue the work begun by Jesus.

The Task Continues

In one sense the New Testament presents all the information we need to know about Jesus—and not only information but a first-century reflection on how Jesus fits into God's revelation and his plan for the history of the world. Here we have a privileged witness to Jesus and to the spread of the good news. But there comes a point when simply reading and re-reading the New

Testament is not enough. Like Mary, the believer must ponder these words in his or her heart, and then seek the help of the faith community to know if one has understood them correctly. As Mary pondered the words and events before and after the birth of Jesus, she came to new understandings about God, herself, and others. The following chapter will show how those three sets of images are interrelated.

For Personal Reflection

1. Have I ever used my God-given gifts against the faith community to which I belong? How did I come to realize that? What changes did I make?
2. Have I ever read the Letter to James in a single sitting? Is today a good day for doing that?
3. What have I treasured and pondered in my heart? Have the treasuring and the pondering made my life any more open to God's grace? In what way?
4. Have I taken from the Prodigal Son parable what Jesus hoped the Pharisees would take from it? Do I sympathize with the elder brother's complaint? Do I see its limitations?
5. Do I tend to recognize God in men and women who "have it all together"? Do I have trouble recognizing God in people whose lives are fragmented and broken? Why or why not?

For Group Discussion

1. Why are we often attracted to, and yet nervous about, Jesus as a crucified savior?
2. Any idea of a monopoly on the charisms needed in the church is a subtle form of idolatry, an attempt to make God into one's own image. Is that statement true? Is it overstating the situation? What difference does all this make, anyway?
3. If we picture all Pharisees as hypocrites, we distort the New Testament and run the risk of using God to justify our self-

interest. Where does honest observance of God's laws end and a cozy legalism begin? How can we know if we have passed from one to the other?

4. Have you ever had an Emmaus experience, where someone walked with you, trying to help you untangle various images of God, and then suddenly everything became clear? Have you been willing to offer the same help to someone in similar circumstances?

5. The Christians for whom Matthew wrote apparently felt caught between the Mosaic Law they had cherished and Jesus' message, which went beyond that Law. Have you ever felt caught between two things you valued and which could not be equally honored at the same time? How did you handle the situation? What advice would you give to someone in similar circumstances?

Further Resources

Raymond Brown, S.S., *The Critical Meaning of the Bible* (Mahwah, NJ: Paulist Press, 1981).

Raymond Brown, S.S., *Biblical Reflections on Crises Facing the Church* (Mahwah, NJ: Paulist Press, 1975). The Pontifical Biblical Commission's "Instruction on the Historical Truth of the Gospels" (April 1964) can be found in this volume as an appendix to Brown's text. According to this Instruction, the gospels went through three stages of development: what Jesus did and said, what eyewitness disciples incorporated into their preaching, and what the writers of the gospels used in their accounts.

Walter Burghardt, S.J., *Lovely in Eyes Not His: Homilies for an Imaging of Christ* (Mahwah, NJ: Paulist Press, 1988).

Terrance Callan, *Forgetting the Root: The Emergence of Christianity from Judaism* (Mahwah, NJ: Paulist Press, 1986). After introductory chapters on Jesus' relation to Judaism, and the early church and Judaism, Callan shows how Christianity moved from a conservative Jewish orientation to a liberal Jewish orientation and finally to a liberal Gentile stance, the position that has shaped it decisively at least since the fourth century.

Eugene Fisher, *Faith Without Prejudice: Rebuilding Christian Attitudes Toward Judaism* (Mahwah, NJ: Paulist Press, 1977).

Anthony Gilles, *People of the Way* (Cincinnati, OH: St. Anthony Messenger Press, 1984).

Robert Grant and David Tracy, *A Short History of the Interpretation of the Bible*, rev. ed. (Philadelphia, PA: Fortress Press, 1984).

Robert Karris, O.F.M., *Invitation to Luke: A Commentary on the Gospel of Luke with Complete Text from The Jerusalem Bible* (New York: Doubleday and Company, Inc., 1977).

Pheme Perkins, *Reading the New Testament*, rev. ed. (Mahwah, NJ: Paulist Press, 1988).

Donald Senior, C.P., *Invitation to Matthew: A Commentary on the Gospel of Matthew with Complete Text from The Jerusalem Bible* (New York: Doubleday and Company, Inc., 1977).

FOUR

Images of God, Ourselves, and Others: What Relation?

In Flannery O'Connor's short story "Revelation," Mrs. Turpin dominates the conversation in a doctor's waiting room as she and her husband Claud wait to see the doctor. As she looks at the others in the waiting room, she notices a fat girl who scowls whenever she looks up from the book she is reading. The girl's mother "had on a yellow sweat shirt and wine-colored slacks, both gritty-looking, and the rims of her lips were stained with snuff. Her dirty yellow hair was tied behind with a little piece of red paper ribbon. Worse than niggers any day, Mrs. Turpin thought."[1]

When the conversation turns to farming, one woman observes that she wouldn't want to raise pigs. Mrs. Turpin says that hers are very clean because the pig parlor has a concrete floor and every day the pigs are hosed down. She is quite happy that God made the world the way it is, and herself so grateful and ready to help everyone. Finally the fat girl throws her book at Mrs. Turpin and attacks her. After the commotion subsides and Mrs. Turpin has taken stock of the bruise on her forehead and the welts around her neck, she asks the girl, "What you got to say to me?" The girl responds, "Go back to hell where you came from, you old wart hog." Shaken, Mrs. Turpin ponders that command for the rest of the afternoon. When she relates the incident to the black women who come to pick cotton, they affirm that she is the sweetest and prettiest white lady they know. "Jesus satisfied with her!" they conclude. But still Mrs. Turpin continues to probe the meaning of this incident.

As she washes down the pigs that evening, Mrs. Turpin asks, "What did you send me a message like that for? How am I a hog and me both? How am I saved and from hell too?" She continues, "It's no trash around here, black or white, that I haven't given to. And break my back to the bone every day working. And do for the church. . . . If you like trash better, go get yourself some trash then. You could have made me trash. Or a nigger. If trash is what you wanted why didn't you make me trash?" Suddenly she has a vision of a wide road leading to heaven, and on it are "whole companies of white-trash, clean for the first time in their lives, and bands of black niggers in white robes, and battalions of freaks and lunatics shouting and clapping and leaping like frogs." At the end of the procession are respectable people like Mrs. Turpin and Claud, "accountable as they had always been for good order and common sense and respectable behavior. They alone were on key. Yet she could see by their shocked and altered faces that even their virtues were being burned away." Shaken by what she sees, she turns off the faucet in the pig parlor and walks back to the house, "but what she heard were the voices of the souls climbing upward into the starry field and shouting hallelujah."

Our images of God do not exist in a vacuum; they are connected to our own self-image and the way we see other people. The girl who threw the book at Mrs. Turpin challenged the smugness that passed judgment on everyone in that waiting room. The fact that Mrs. Turpin questioned God in prayer about this incident indicates that she was not quite as sure of things as she pretended to be. She walked into the doctor's waiting room sure of God, herself, and other people; she left that waiting room with troubling questions about all three. Even after her welts had disappeared, those questions remained.

What Price Conversion?

Part of our difficulty in adjusting our images of God is that in the process we must adjust our self-image and the way we see other people. If we congratulate ourselves on having God all figured out (like the Pharisee in the Temple), then we are probably also pleased with our own self-image and confident that we understand other people, especially those who might try unsuccessfully to trick us.

How can I grow in my images of God if I am completely self-satisfied? Where is the room to convert? Where is the readiness to admit that the world is bigger than my little categories? What more could the Pharisee praying in the front of the Temple learn about God, himself, or people like that despicable tax collector in the back of the Temple?

When Jesus asked those condemned why they had refused to help him when he was hungry, naked, and in prison, they were surprised by the question, for they considered themselves quite pious. When those who were saved asked when they had done all these works of mercy on God's behalf, they heard that every time they fed the hungry, clothed the naked, and visited the

sick or those in prison, they had offered these works of
mercy to Jesus.

Our images of God, self, and others interconnect.
Mrs. Turpin in the doctor's waiting room and the Pharisee in the Temple have no trouble thanking God for
not making them like certain people. Both thank God
that they are not like some despised group; both pride
themselves on figuring out the world and not being deceived by anyone. Their smugness does not strike them
as sinful; they think they see things as God sees them.

The Habit of Being, the collected letters of Flannery
O'Connor, contains several letters to A., a friend who
was considering becoming a Catholic. In an 8 September 1955 letter, O'Connor compares such a decision to
marriage.

> When you get into it, you find it is the begin-
> ning, not the end, of the struggle to make love
> work. I think most people come to the Church
> by means the Church does not allow; else there
> would be no need their getting to her at all. How-
> ever, this is true inside as well, as the operation of
> the Church is entirely set up for the sinner; which
> creates much misunderstanding among the
> smug.[2]

In the end, Mrs. Turpin might have agreed with that
comment.

In another letter to A., O'Connor describes smugness as "the Great Catholic Sin."

> I find it in myself and don't dislike it any less.
> One reason Guardini is a relief to read is that
> he has nothing of it. With a few exceptions the
> American clergy, when it takes to the pen, brings
> this particular sin with it in full force.[3]

Those who suffer from smugness regarding their images
of God, self, and others do not feel a pressing need for

conversion; they have assured themselves they are simply being realistic.

Whatever lenses a person uses to see God will be used to see oneself and others. The Pharisee in the Temple and those condemned in the last judgment parable did not consciously think about that interrelation, but they put it into practice nonetheless. The good Samaritan and those saved in the same last judgment parable did not talk constantly about this interconnection of images, but they show its positive expression.

Men and women become adults spiritually as they begin to recognize that their images of God fall short of the reality. They see how easily those images can be biased in their own favor or against certain groups of people. Not all of them have experiences as dramatic as Mrs. Turpin's, but they all come to question their complacency.

Genuine conversion is neither quick nor painless. It never pretends that the necessary self-sacrifice will touch only peripheral areas of one's life. Genuine conversion demands that we surrender our idols (for example, a God domesticated to our standards, a deceptive self-image, a tendency to see ourselves always on the side of the angels) and accept life on God's terms. Those terms tend to be both more generous and more demanding than our terms; they cannot be fully accepted in one dramatic moment of conversion. Several stories about holy men and women illustrate the never-ending process of conversion.

Augustine of Hippo wrote his *Confessions* as an account of all the ways God tried to reach him and how obtuse he had remained to God's designs, how zealously he had constructed a world according to his own liking, according to his own notion of self-sacrifice.[4] And yet even when Augustine received baptism at the age of 39, his process of conversion was far from complete.

Toward the end of his life, Francis of Assisi wrote a testament for his brothers; there he recounts how, as a young man, "it seemed very bitter to me to see lepers. And the Lord led me among them and I had mercy upon them. And when I left them that which seemed bitter to me was changed into sweetness of soul and body; and afterward I lingered a little and left the world."[5]

This remembrance compresses a number of incidents, the most famous of which happened while Francis was riding outside Assisi and unexpectedly encountered a man suffering from leprosy. Already questioning some of his images of God, himself, and others, Francis leapt off his horse and embraced the man. That action did not cure the man's leprosy, but it started to cure Francis' narrow vision about how God acts and does not act in daily life. Eventually Francis and those who followed him devoted a good deal of time to caring for men and women suffering from leprosy. In doing so, they challenged the conventional wisdom of their day, especially the idea that leprosy is a punishment from God. Embracing that man on the road outside Assisi would have been a superficial act if Francis had not sought out others suffering from this dreaded disease, ministering to their material and spiritual needs. The incident on the road represents a part, not the whole, of Francis' conversion. His values were turned upside down; the terms "bitter" and "sweet" exchanged places as new images of God, himself, and others took shape.

Francis left the world in the sense that he left behind the world he knew best, the world where rising middle-class merchants like his father were replacing the older aristocracy as the movers and shakers of society. Francis did not leave the world in the sense that he now despised the society to which he owed so much. He did not leave the world in the sense that he was now sinless and had left all temptations behind. Indeed, not long before he died Francis urged his friars, "Let us begin to serve the Lord God, for up to now we have made little or no progress."[6]

In "Challenge to the Church: A Theological Comment on the Political Crisis in South Africa" (also called the *Kairos Document* of 1985), 150 Christian theologians in that country described the *kairos*, or moment of truth and decision, Christians there face.[7] The interrelation of images of God, self, and others is evident.

> Both oppressor and oppressed claim loyalty to the same Church. They are both baptized in the same baptism and participate together in the same bread, the same body and blood of Christ. There we sit in the same Church while outside Christian policemen and soldiers are beating up and killing Christian children or torturing Christian prisoners to death while yet other Christians stand by and weakly plead for peace.[8]

The authors describe the South African government as having a "state theology" that is, in reality, "simply the theological justification of the status quo with its racism, capitalism, and totalitarianism." A misuse of Romans 13:1–7 ("Everyone is to obey the governing authorities, because there is no authority except from God") plays a key role in such theology by appearing to give divine approval to oppressive governments. The authors of the *Kairos Document* note that every biblical text "must be interpreted in its context" and that the context of Paul's teaching in Romans does not support such an interpretation. The authors later refer to the "blasphemous use of God's holy name in the preamble to the new apartheid constitution," which reads:

In humble submission to Almighty God, who
controls the destinies of nations and the history
of peoples; who gathered our forebears together
from many lands and gave them this their own;
who has guided them from generation to generation; who has wondrously delivered them from
the dangers that beset them ... [9]

According to the authors of the *Kairos Document*,

This god is an idol. It is as mischievous, sinister
and evil as any of the idols that the prophets
of Israel had to contend with. Here we have a
god who is historically on the side of the white
settlers, who dispossesses black people of their
land and who gives the major part of the land to
his "chosen people." [10]

Such a god exalts the proud and humbles the poor, the
very opposite of the God Mary described in her *Magnificat*.

In analyzing what they call church theology, the
authors sharply criticize appeals for

reconciliation, without admitting the need for
justice,
justice, but not challenging the structural injustice of South African society,
and for non-violence—as though the pass laws,
forcible removal to "homelands" and discrim-
ination in jobs, education and housing are not
a form of violence. [11]

The authors of the *Kairos Document* criticize a totally in-
dividualistic and other-worldly spirituality; they call for
a prophetic spirituality unafraid to point out where injustice exists and where repentance is needed.

In 1986 a group of evangelical Christians belonging to charismatic and pentecostal churches and groups
wrote "Evangelical Witness in South Africa." Their goal

was to critique evangelical theology and practice and "to turn it into an effective evangelical witness in South Africa today."[12] Images of God, self, and others, images popular among some evangelical Christians, are called into question by the authors of this document.

> We wish to confess that our evangelical family has a track record of supporting and legitimating oppressive regimes here and elsewhere. That this family has tended to assume conservative positions which tend to maintain the status quo.
> We wish to confess that the people who regard themselves as evangelicals across all the churches in South Africa condemn and campaign against all efforts to change the racist apartheid system in South Africa.[13]

After criticizing an unbiblical dualism (heavenly things matter/earthly things do not), the authors lament that within the evangelical tradition "those we thought were the ones who are 'born again' and 'reconciled' to God have turned out to be the worst racists, oppressors, and exploiters."[14]

The authors criticize a fundamentalistic use of Romans 13:1–7 without regard for its context within Paul's teaching. After describing the preamble of the South African constitution (quoted above) as "blasphemous," they say that this God

> comes across as the god of the oppressor to black people in South Africa. It is a 'God' of the white people of South Africa. To the township youths who are attacked and killed, this 'God' is the god of the teargas, bullets, sjamboks, prison cells and death. This type of God to us Christians comes across as an antichrist, negating the very basis of our Christian faith.[15]

Later these evangelical authors criticize evangelical groups that come into South Africa, especially from the United States, to preach a God little interested in social justice but very worried about the spread of communism. According to the South African evangelicals, "these tendencies have reinforced the perceptions of some blacks that God is a God of the white oppressors and that the church is a western institution used by the western countries to keep blacks in subjugation."[16] Lamenting a less than radical approach to repentance, the authors observe:

> The problem with us [evangelicals] is that we became very radical and uncompromising against a well-selected set of sins while ignoring the rest for reasons that are not clear to many. We preach vociferously against adultery, fornication, drunkenness, thieves, robbers, hatred but are completely silent about the sin of discrimination and the sin of apartheid.[17]

Whites, they say, "can remain racists who undermine and dehumanize blacks and still be regarded as 'fantastic' Christians."

Conversion in our images of God, self, and others is neither cheap nor painless; we have invested a great deal in believing that our images of all three are correct. Any significant re-evaluation of one of those images automatically involves re-examining the other two.

The character Javert in the Broadway musical *Les Miserables*, based on Victor Hugo's novel, illustrates the interlocking nature of those images and the price of conversion. In the Broadway production the musical opens with Javert, a police commissioner, giving parole papers to Jean Valjean, a man who served nineteen years in prison for stealing a loaf of bread. The former prisoner must present those papers on seeking employment or doing anything that requires government recognition. Valjean soon finds that employers will not hire anyone who has been in prison. He is tempted to despair of God, himself, and everyone else, when, on meeting the kindly bishop of Digne, Valjean is fed and given shelter. He decides to steal some silverware and leave during the night. Apprehended by the police, he is brought back to the bishop who says that he gave Valjean the silverware and also a pair of candlesticks Valjean had forgotten to take. The former prisoner soon destroys his parole papers, assumes a new identity, becoming a factory owner and mayor of his town. At this point Javert, the policeman, loses track of Valjean.

Eight years later Valjean meets Javert, who does not recognize him. A runaway horse, however, upsets a huge cart, which pins an innocent man. Valjean is inclined to help the man but fears that Javert may recognize his uncommon strength and remember prisoner 24601. When Valjean takes the risk, Javert does recognize him and refuses to hear about Valjean's new life. "Men like you can never change," snarls Javert.[18] Valjean manages to escape and begins to raise Cosette, the orphaned daughter of one of his factory workers. Nine years later Javert, still looking for prisoner 24601, rescues Valjean and Cosette from a street gang but fails to recognize them until it is too late. He promptly vows to catch Valjean. Javert sings a personal credo as he affirms, "Mine is the way of the Lord, and those who follow the path of the righteous shall have their reward." Javert praises the stars for filling the darkness with order and light and for always being the same. He adds, "It is written on the doorway to paradise that those who falter and fall must pay the price. Lord, let me find him that I may see him safe behind bars. I will never rest until then—this I swear by the stars."[19]

Talk of revolution soon fills the Parisian air, with Valjean helping the rebellious students and Javert working as an undercover policeman. Attempting to lead the students into a trap, Javert is discovered and is summarily sentenced to be executed. Just then the students must return to the barricades. Valjean spares Javert. Shaken by that experience, Javert stands on a Paris bridge on a bright, starry night, making a counter-profession of faith, utterly shattered that Valjean has turned out to be not a criminal but a decent, generous human being. Javert commits suicide by jumping off the bridge.

While Jean Valjean's images of God, self, and others are becoming more whole, Javert nurtures a parody of all three images. Confronted with that caricature, he commits suicide rather than change. His earlier prayerful vow to find Valjean turns out to be not a prayer at all, but rather a hymn to a tidy "god" whom self-righteous people like Javert can completely understand and manipulate.

Conversion—Never Finished This Side of Heaven

It is always dangerous to say, "Mine is the way of the Lord." Such language suggests that we have already fully converted. In fact, discipleship is never finished until we see God face to face at the moment of death. True, we may make major decisions that orient us to the Lord's ways, but it is smaller, more ordinary, daily choices that implement and solidify those major decisions. None of this brings God's ways under the individual's control.

Saintly men, women, and children remain open to God's grace; they do their work in faithfulness and pray with increasing generosity. Conversion should lead us to the day when we will see God "face to face." Short of that day, however, we have no room for total rest, no room to consider our conversion final.

Our conversion is not finished this side of heaven, but in honest, persevering prayer this conversion takes deeper root and shows us how our images of God, self, and others are interrelated. The next chapter will show how our images of God, with their connections to self-image and images of others, are related to our prayer.

For Personal Reflection

1. Have I ever had anyone rudely challenge my images of God, self, and others? How did that challenge affect those images?
2. Have I ever seen my values turned upside down, with what seemed bitter becoming sweet and what seemed sweet becoming bitter? How did I consolidate my new values?
3. Have I ever complained that someone who claimed to be preaching the good news of Jesus was simply making a political statement? Was some vested interest of mine being threatened? Is it still being threatened?
4. What can someone like Valjean, the former prisoner, say to me about conversion? about forgiveness?
5. Have I ever struggled to forgive someone and then found myself unexpectedly freed of anger and resentment? Am I still struggling with a decision to forgive someone? What is holding me back?
6. Were any of my decisions yesterday insignificant in the eyes of God? Will any of today's decisions be insignificant?

For Group Discussion

1. Whether we like it or not, our images of God, self, and others are interrelated. Why is that so?
2. Why are genuine conversions always continuous?
3. A group of evangelical Christians in South Africa has criticized their own religious group for firmly denouncing one set of sins while tending to ignore other sins. In what way is such one-sided denunciation a common temptation among the followers of Jesus?
4. Can I point to historical examples where some individual

or group tried to use Christianity to support anti-Christian attitudes? Did that attempt succeed or fail?

5. When Javert the policeman says, "Men like you can never change," is he describing the former prisoner or himself? Does his use of the expression "men like you" suggest Javert's own resistance to personal conversion? How common or rare is that approach to life?

6. In prayer we acknowledge God's grace and our freedom. Both have profound implications for the way we live. Have we sometimes feared honest prayer because we instinctively feared its consequences?

Further Resources

Albert Nolan, O.P., *God in South Africa: The Challenge of the Gospel* (Grand Rapids, MI: Wm. B. Eerdmans Publishing Co., 1988).

Philip Sheldrake, *Images of Holiness* (Notre Dame, IN: Ave Maria Press, 1988).

Richard Sweeney, *Spirituality and the Seasons of Adulthood* audiocassette (Cincinnati, OH: St. Anthony Messenger Press, 1987).

Jean Vanier, *Be Not Afraid* (Mahwah, NJ: Paulist Press, 1975).

Elie Wiesel, *Four Hasidic Masters and Their Struggle Against Melancholy* (Notre Dame, IN: University of Notre Dame Press, 1978).

FIVE

Prayer and Our Images of God

How many of us turn to God when we face what we regard as a personal failure (failing a course at school, not getting a certain job, becoming unemployed), a family crisis (death, chemical dependence, estrangement from parents or children), or some other difficulty? And when we pray, what kind of a God do we meet? What kind of expectations do we bring to this encounter?

Those questions became very vivid for me that day during my junior year in high school when twin nephews were born prematurely and died a few days later. That short time was long enough for me to embark on the most serious praying I had ever done in my life. Friends and family members also prayed for those two infants. This wasn't the first time I ever asked God for something, but it was the first life-and-death petition I had ever brought to God. After a couple days of such praying, I felt fairly confident that my nephews were going to win their struggle against all the odds. When they died, I was crushed. And, of course, so were many other people.

What image of God had I brought to my prayer? Would I take away from this experience the same image of God? If not, how would the new image differ?

Would God become more aloof, less interested in the faith-problems of a seventeen-year-old? How could I continue to believe that God was good and all-loving when things like this happen? Life is never the same after such a loss, and future prayers are certainly influenced by such an experience.

Prayer and Sorting Out Our Images of God

A tragedy such as I experienced (and I now realize that many people experience more painful ones at a much younger age) does not lead to a single conclusion. One person may decide that there is no God; another may decide that he or she failed to say the correct prayers or should have vowed to do some good work if the tragedy were averted. A third person might go back to the drawing board, so to speak, and start sorting out his or her images of God.

After my nephews died, I was sorting out my images of God for months, wanting to believe that God is good, that God cares as much about newborn infants as about keeping all creation in existence, and yet I did not know how to reconcile that belief with the stark reality that my nephews had died.

Eventually I realized that I had prayed in a somewhat pagan fashion: God, here's the problem, here's what I expect you to do about it, now go do it. I had used prayer to back God into a corner; he would have to respond as I considered best and according to my timetable. God was there to be flattered, cajoled, and bribed if need be. My prayer was to catch God's attention and change his mind about those prematurely born twins.

It could have been worse. In similar circumstances some people turn to chain prayers (the homemade kind you sometimes find left behind in church pews) or to so-called guaranteed prayers, a certain devotion will assure the desired outcome. In a strange way such prayers end up treating God either as absentminded or as slightly malicious, though capable of being straightened out.

Pagan prayers try to catch the attention of a very busy God or make "an offer he can't refuse." Such was the prayer of the Pharisee in the Temple, who seemed slightly afraid that some of the wonderful things he was doing for God (fasting twice a week, paying tithes on everything he owned) might have escaped God's notice. The Pharisee thanked God that he was not like other people, even like the tax collector.

There is a strange ecumenism at work in this story. Jews, Christians, and non-Christians are all very capable of praying selfishly, as though the person is the fixed point and God is the one who changes.

But there is another way I can pray, which arises from a different approach to God: I pray not to change God's mind but rather to bring my life, including my sufferings, into harmony with God's grace. Such was the approach of the tax collector, who stood at the back of the Temple, beating his breast and praying, "O God, be merciful to me, a sinner." If I pray in this way, God is the fixed point, and I am the one who changes. Conversion, therefore, is the result of seeing God—and thus myself and other people—more clearly and being willing to change my life accordingly.

Perhaps it seems terribly obvious to say that my images of God and my willingness to grow in those images will determine how I pray and how I will deal with what happens after I pray. Based on my personal experience and my years of priestly ministry, I am convinced that the difficulties many people face in prayer cannot be resolved until they face the images of God on which their prayers are based. Those images have very radical implications for how the praying person sees himself or herself and others. The Pharisee and the tax collector in the Temple differed in all three images (God, self, others). This chapter examines the images of God as reflected in one's prayer; those images, of course, are related to a person's self-image and image of others.

Biblical Examples of
Men and Women Whose Images of God Grew

In the Book of Genesis we find two prayers of Jacob, separated by at least twenty years, which illustrate how prayer changes as one's image of God changes. Soon after Jacob deprives Esau of his birthright, Jacob flees to Haran where his uncle Laban lives. Jacob has a vision of a ladder with angels going up and down. Then God says that Jacob's descendants will be as plentiful as the dust on the ground and that they will possess this land. Exclaiming that this place is nothing less than the abode of God and the gate of heaven, Jacob sets up a pillar, anoints it with oil, and renames the place Bethel (House of God). Then he vows:

> If God remains with me and keeps me safe on the journey I am making, if he gives me food to eat and clothes to wear, and if I come home safe to my father's home, then Yahweh shall be my God. This stone I have set up as a pillar is to be a house of God, and I shall faithfully pay you a tenth part of everything you give me (Gn 28:20–22).

After many years Jacob decides to return to Canaan. When the messengers he sent to Esau return with the news that Esau is approaching with four hundred men, Jacob fears that Esau is seeking revenge. He prays:

> God of my father Abraham, and God of my father Isaac, Yahweh who told me, "Go back to your native land and I will be good to you," I am

unworthy of all the faithful love and constancy you have shown your servant. I had only my staff when I crossed this Jordan, and now I have grown into two camps. I implore you, save me from my brother Esau's clutches, for I am afraid that he may come and attack me, mothers and children alike. Yet it was you who said, "I shall be very good to you, and make your descendants like the sand of the sea, which is too numerous to count" (Gn 32:10–13).

The Jacob who prays this second prayer is older and wiser than the Jacob who promises that Yahweh will be his god if Yahweh brings him safely back to Canaan. The older Jacob prays differently because he has a different image of God, one that can admit that Jacob is quite unworthy of the faithful love and constancy Yahweh has shown to him. With some justification we could say that the younger Jacob prayed like the Pharisee in the Temple and the older Jacob prayed like the tax collector. Jacob's two prayers reflect different images of God and of himself—in this case the second image is closer to the truth.

I am indebted to John Sanford for pointing out the growth in Jacob's image of God and in his prayers.[1] Sanford also points out a similar growth in the prayers of Joseph and Moses.

While the prayers of Jacob reflect an improvement in his image of God, the story of Solomon cautions against believing that progress in this area is inevitable. When Solomon began his reign as king, he asked for "a heart to understand how to govern your people, how to discern between good and evil" (1 Kgs 3:9). By the time Solomon died, he had compromised his belief in the God of Abraham, Isaac, and Jacob by erecting shrines and temples to various pagan gods worshipped by his wives and by Solomon himself. The story of Solomon shows that because conversion is always possible, the possibility of regression remains.

Other examples of biblical men and women whose image of God grew as they persevered in prayer include Hosea, Jeremiah, and the author of the Book of Wisdom. Judith, Esther, and Tobit know that God is their only security; they grow in their image of God as their trials mount despite their faith in God.

Perhaps no one in the Hebrew scriptures prayed as roughly as Job did or experienced a comparable growth in his understanding of God. Although we might consider Job's complaints, his insistence that God come into court and defend the way he runs the world, as a lack of faith, all Job's speeches represent a way of praying, a way of realizing that one's previous images of God were inadequate.

Whether we talk about personal growth from a physical, mental, emotional, or social perspective, we are talking about something that can be messy, that has rough edges, and that may not feel like growth while we are in the midst of it. I believe the same can be said for the way we grow in our images of God. The author of the Suffering Servant songs in Second Isaiah may not have felt any growth in his images of God, but the way those four passages challenge the idea that all suffering is a sign of God's disapproval can only be described as a breakthrough and as a tremendous theological advance in the Hebrew scriptures.

Probably not one of the biblical men or women cited above set out to grow in his or her images of God. But all of them were ready to move beyond tidy, comfortable images toward images more capable of doing justice to God's immense love, mercy, and desire that men and women share in the divine life for which they have been created. They all prayed with a deepening honesty about themselves and the God they served. Instead, any one of them might have complained that God's ways are not fair and stomped off in a self-righteous huff.

In the New Testament accounts of Jesus' temptation in the desert, we meet a tempter who offers a plausible image of God to make each suggested action (turning stones into bread, jumping off the Temple parapet, worshipping the tempter) seem pious. The tempter uses scripture to legitimate these images of God, but Jesus demolishes the too-neat, too-comfortable images of God offered by the tempter by citing other scripture verses that suggest wider and more risky images of God. Such a God does not guarantee riches, prestige, or worldly success; such a God is worshipped for his own sake and not because the worshipper prays in order to create an obligation, which God must then honor.

Blinded on the road to Damascus, Saul of Tarsus' images of God were turned upside down. The God Saul thought he was serving so faithfully and so zealously asked why Saul was persecuting him. Prayer and openness to larger images of God must have been a major part of the early days of Saul's conversion—not to mention his many years as a preacher of the good news of Jesus. Paul later had to defend that good news from other Christians whose images of God excluded gentile Christians who did not observe the Law of Moses.

People whose images of God are being challenged by current events (world problems, family crises, personal suffering) may not feel like praying. But only if they pray honestly will they ever come to see that God surpasses their previous images—however advanced those images may have seemed.

For this reason, at times we may have to pray in anger. We may have to voice our sense of betrayal, our

sense of being treated unfairly, and our sense of helpless-
ness before we can see that our anger usually arises from
images of God that were impoverished in relation to the
images of God presented in the scriptures and brought to
life through the lives of holy men and women in every
time and place.[2]

Holy Men and Women
Whose Images of God Grew in Prayer

In the age of microwaves, direct dial phone calls,
and live TV coverage worldwide, we are increasingly
tempted to think that religious conversions happen in an
instant, somehow assuring their recipients of a happy,
holy life from that point forward. Rarely do we visualize
holy men and women continuing to grow in their images of God, sometimes even praying in anger during
the "growing pains" prior to a more honest, generous—
and risky!—image of God. Often we suspect that their
prayers are totally serene, without any difficult moments
or rough edges. Thus we simultaneously honor holy men
and women and neutralize their good example by seeing in them a painless perfection we cannot relate to our
own lives, especially to our prayers.

It's easy to think that people such as Mother Teresa
of Calcutta or Brother Roger of Taize have been left on
this earth to give us lesser mortals striking models of
heroic virtue. At any given moment there are a few
widely-acclaimed holy people, and a far greater number less well known—and I believe that not one of them
"has it made," has passed beyond the need to grow in
his or her images of God, or has a prayer life with never
a rough edge or difficult moment. Perhaps a closer look
at the lives of several holy men and women will explain
this dynamic.

Francis of Assisi (1182–1226) may be one of the
most romanticized saints in the Catholic church. True,

his life had its moments of high drama (embracing the man suffering from leprosy, renouncing his inheritance and returning all his clothes to his father, meeting Sultan Al-Maliak al-Kamil in Egypt and preaching to him about Jesus Christ, convincing a pope to authorize a revolutionary form of religious life, receiving the marks of Christ's passion, and so forth), but there was also a highly contemplative Francis, a Francis whose conversion process lasted at least three years in its most obvious phase, a Francis who did not always pray with the consolation that he had understood God's will or that he had sufficient talent or courage to put that will into practice. The dramatic moments in Francis' life easily lend themselves to painting, sculpture, songs, plays, or films, but how easily can artists or dramatists show us a Francis who needed and continued to grow in his images of God until the day he died? Francis with the Christmas crib at Greccio or taming the wolf of Gubbio is more easily dramatized than Francis praying in cold caves, asking God for guidance about how to lead an order that had grown astronomically and threatened to split into many factions. The Canticle of the Creatures is more easily set to music or painted than Francis' saying toward the end of his life, "Brothers, let us begin to serve the Lord God, for up to now we have made little or no progress." Few people realize what physical suffering and spiritual struggles preceded the composition of that hymn to God's goodness.

The "birdbath St. Francis" shows him blessing birds or deer, not struggling with his own demons or trying to call people to their own responsibility to be holy rather than basking in the perceived holiness of someone else.

Francis' "perfect joy" story may offer some clues about how his images of God grew in prayer. One day as he was travelling with Brother Leo, his secretary, Francis said that he would not consider it perfect joy if someone rushed up to say that all the masters of theology in Paris, the most prestigious theological school at that time, had suddenly decided to become Friars Minor (members of the order Francis founded). Later Francis said he would not consider it perfect joy if someone else informed him that all the bishops of the church or the kings of England and France had decided to enter the Franciscan order. Francis explained that perfect joy would not be the news that the friars had converted all the non-Christians in the whole world or that they had received the gift of miracles. At this point an exasperated Brother Leo asked what Francis *would* consider perfect joy. Francis said that if the two of them, hungry and freezing, arrived at their headquarters and the porter failed to recognize them, and called them robbers and beat them with a stick, drove them back into the cold and rain—if, for the love of God, they could endure all these things without losing their patience and charity, that would be perfect joy.[3]

An inspiring story but what does it tell us about Francis, his prayer, and his images of God? First of all, the story has some common elements with chapter 13 of First Corinthians ("If I should give my body to be burned but have not love . . ."). Neither Paul nor Francis could have recognized the dead ends mistaken for perfect love or perfect joy without the help of honest and persevering prayer, which purges us of false images of God and of ourselves. Second, in telling us what might be mistaken for perfect joy, Francis may very well have been repeating some of the temptations he had experienced—much as Christ was tempted in the desert by half-truths. Third, the Francis who told this story was somewhat close to the end of his life; he was not a twenty-two-year-old who had recently heard the crucifix at the run-down church of San Damiano tell him to go rebuild the church. It took

Francis some months and much hard work to rebuild the chapel of San Damiano, but it would take much longer and much harder work to make his contribution to rebuilding the larger church.

The images of God that Francis had at age twenty-two were important, but they were not the only images Francis would ever have, and they were not necessarily the images that would sustain him in his most difficult moments. Nor did those sustaining images drop down from heaven; they were discovered, appreciated, and refined, especially through prayer.

Another story about St. Francis may offer more insight into his prayer life and his images of God. Once when Francis was upset over the bad example given by some of his followers, he prayed and God asked him, "Why are you disturbed, little man? Did I not place you over my order as its shepherd, and now you do not know that I am its chief protector?" God said that Francis should not act as though everything depended on his human efforts.[4] Where did Francis receive that answer? In honest prayer, in a prayer unafraid to hide his frustration. This incident shows that a mistaken image of God has immediate implications for the way a person views himself or herself and others. Francis never said that he prayed in anger, but I find it difficult to understand how anger could have been completely absent from the prayers that underlie the "perfect joy" story and the "little man" story.

At times we are tempted to make holy men and women some kind of "spiritual Rambos," capable of battling the most deadly, subtle sins through sheer force of will. Of course the movie Rambo always has a very clear, external enemy; Rambo is never part of the problem. Like the tax collector at the back of the Temple, holy men and women know that they are part of the problem

—no matter how much, by the grace of God, they may also be part of the remedy. Francis certainly helped rebuild the church, but he also contributed to its need for rebuilding. And he never forgot that.

Teresa of Avila (1515–82) came from a wealthy family, entered the Carmelite monastery of the Incarnation, a large, wealthy monastery for the daughters of the nobility, in 1536 and spent her first fourteen years there as a rather pampered nun. Her prayer life was quite difficult until, at the age of thirty-nine, she had two conversion experiences: one on seeing a statue of the suffering Christ, and the other on reading the *Confessions* of St. Augustine. Her prayer became less self-centered and more open to God's direction.[5]

Eight years later Teresa founded San Jose, her first reformed monastery of Carmelite nuns—eleven of them living in a poor house, doing their own cooking, manual labor, and dedicating themselves to private and communal prayer. Soon she and another Carmelite, John of the Cross, were establishing reformed monasteries of Carmelite nuns and monks. No stranger to opposition in this work, she had to explain her work to fellow Carmelites, bishops, royalty, and representatives of the pope. Not all these people were sure that Teresa's work was inspired by God. In persevering prayer she came to know the Lord more closely and found the strength to continue her work.

Teresa's prayer was usually directed to "his Majesty," her favorite title for Jesus Christ. In *The Way of Perfection*, a book about prayer written for the nuns at San Jose, Teresa advises them to avoid false humility and to act toward God "as toward a father or a brother, as toward your lord or your spouse. Think of Him sometimes under one such aspect, and sometimes under another."[6] Teresa was describing a style of prayer open to many images of God. Eventually those images of God (and of ourselves) give way, she says, to complete openness to God, who is beyond any attempt to apprehend or possess him. Once when Teresa was complaining in prayer about her trials and sufferings, the Lord told her, "Teresa, so do I treat My friends." She crisply responded, "That's why you have so few friends."[7]

At one point in *The Way of Perfection*, Teresa describes the danger of having such an inflated self-image that one is easily offended and forever engaged in defending one's honor, one's prestige. What kind of God is endlessly concerned with questions of prestige? What kind of people are we if our attempts to vindicate ourselves in relation to real or supposed enemies undermine our prayer? Only a willingness to rethink our images of God, as well as our images of ourselves and others, can promote an honest, prayerful interrelation of these images.

Frederick Ozanam (1813–53) founded the St. Vincent de Paul Society to aid the sick, the homeless, and the hungry. He saw in them an image of God that was not being respected by many people, including many Catholics.[8] Frederick's growth in faith was neither linear nor inevitable. As a young man at Lyons College, he had doubts about his faith. Prayer and reading did not seem to help as much as long walks and discussions with a priest-friend. Frederick wanted to study literature, but his father insisted that he study law, which he did. At the Sorbonne University, Frederick encountered several professors whose lectures included sharp challenges to Catholic teaching. Frederick responded by organizing a discussion club where Catholics, atheists, and agnostics could debate the issues of the day. One day, after Frederick had made a grand defense of Christianity's contribution to civilization, one of the club's members responded, "Let us be frank, Mr. Ozanam; let us also be very particular. What do you do besides talk to prove the faith you claim is in you?"

Frederick was so stung by that question that his images of God began to change. Personal devotions and splendid liturgies have their place, but he realized that the gospel includes concrete acts of charity, like visiting poor people in Paris tenements. The St. Vincent de Paul Society was born when he and a friend began to do this.

After the 1848 revolution the French government asked Frederick and his Vincentians to supervise government aid to the poor. Soon he started *The New Era*, a newspaper dedicated to securing justice for the poor and the working classes. Not all Catholics shared his enthusiasm or convictions on this matter, but Frederick continued doing what he knew to be right. His friend Lacordaire, who preached at Frederick's funeral, called him one of those people "in whom God joins tenderness to genius in order to enkindle the world."

Frederick Ozanam did not leave extensive accounts of his prayer life, but is it likely that he inspired many people to bring their own actions toward the poor into conformity with their faith—that he did this in his own time and inspires others today to do the same—without growing in his images of God? Those images developed in prayer and in the very concrete actions of helping the sick, the homeless, and the hungry. Following the example of the last judgment parable, Frederick saw the image of Jesus in all people, especially the needy. Frederick did not see the Vincentians' work as terribly heroic, and he cautioned his collaborators to be sure that their acts of charity never demeaned the person who received them. The image of God must be respected in each individual.

Dorothy Day (1897–1980) is most famous for founding the *Catholic Worker* (an organization and a newspaper), for setting up soup kitchens and assistance programs in New York City and elsewhere, for her fight against racism in American society and within the Catholic church, and for the way she denounced nuclear idolatry and supported the rights of farm workers.[9] At the height of the Depression, when many were tempted to think that communism was the answer to the world's problems and that the Catholic church was unconcerned about the homeless and the hungry, Dorothy Day showed a holiness not afraid to roll up its sleeves and do what needed to be done—whether the recipient believed in God or not.

Dorothy Day experienced some of the "perfect joy" described by St. Francis when she was verbally abused both by her former communist friends and by her fellow Catholics. In time she was widely respected, but one doesn't cope with trying to get out a newspaper on a shoestring budget, raise a daughter alone, pay the rent on facilities to feed the hungry and shelter the homeless, deal with hate letters, and so forth, thinking that some day all that sacrifice will be appreciated. Her many images of God helped her see the profound implications of Jesus' incarnation. The *Catholic Worker* masthead shows a black worker and a white laborer shaking hands in front of Jesus and a cross. One of Fritz Eicherberg's woodcuts for the *Catholic Worker* shows a cold and hungry Jesus standing in a bread line.

According to Jim Forest, who worked with Dorothy Day for several years:

One good definition of Christian life, certainly that of the Catholic Worker movement, is to say that it is the continual rediscovery of the face of Jesus in those around us, but especially in those

faces in which we are least inclined to search for
it: in the poor, and in our enemies.[10]

Dorothy Day became a holy woman through honest,
persevering prayer (open to seeing one's own idolatries
and to seeing new images of God), and the very practical, daily, sometimes exciting but more often very ordinary corporal and spiritual works of mercy. Her style of
life and her practice of weekly confession suggest that
Dorothy knew her need for lifelong conversion, for admitting her blind spots, and for asking forgiveness of
God and the people she had hurt.

From her religious fervor as a child to her adoles-
cent involvement in the suffragette movement, to her
bohemian and communist phase, to her common-law
marriage and desire to have her daughter baptized a
Catholic, to her own baptism in 1927, and then fifty-three
years of service, writing, and challenging the consciences
of American Catholics and others—in all of this Dorothy
Day was not motivated by a single image of God but
was open to the images of God emerging from accepting
God's forgiveness and from her uncomplaining efforts to
put the gospel into practice. It was no accident that she
entitled her newspaper column "On Pilgrimage."

Bishop Desmond Tutu, the Anglican Archbishop of
Cape Town, South Africa, and winner of the 1984 Nobel
Peace Prize, has denounced before the whole world the
South African government's attempts to make apartheid
look normal.[11] Many of those government officials be-
long to a whites-only section of the Dutch Reformed
Church, a section that considers apartheid to be in har-
mony with the scriptures.

In a 1983 interview with the *London Observer*, Arch-
bishop Tutu described how he met Bishop Trevor
Huddleston, then a young Anglican priest serving in
Sophiatown, a black settlement near Johannesburg. "I

was standing with my mother one day, when this white man in a cassock walked past and doffed his big black hat to her. I couldn't believe it—a white man raising his hat to a simple black labouring woman."[12] When Desmond Tutu was sick with tuberculosis for twenty months in his late teens, Father Huddleston visited him almost daily, giving spiritual assistance and supplying books for this voracious young reader.

Tutu eventually became a high school teacher but resigned after three years when the South African government introduced a state-run system of "Bantu education," designed from the start to be second-rate. At the start of his theological education Tutu says that he was "not moved by very high ideals," but in time his love for scripture and prayer grew and his spiritual motivation deepened.[13] Changing images of God must have been part of that process. After his priestly ordination, parish assignments, further theological education, and his ordination as a bishop, Desmond Tutu became secretary general of the Southern African Council of Churches (SACC), to which the whites-only branches of the Dutch Reformed Church do not belong. When he testified before a government commission investigating the SACC, Bishop Tutu said that his testimony would show that the God whom the members of the SACC worship is very much concerned with children starving in resettlement camps, with people who die mysteriously in detention, and with people banned by the South African government. "I might add," he said, "that if God did not care about these and similar matters, I would not worship Him, for He would be a totally useless God. Mercifully, He is not such a God."[14]

As a result of his activities in South Africa and his statements to the world press, Archbishop Tutu's passport has been revoked twice, his actions have been constantly monitored, and he has received threatening letters and phone calls. Some of his opponents accuse him of being a communist or a communist sympathizer.

One of his favorite stories is that before the whites came to South Africa, "we had the land, and they had the Bible. Then they said, 'Let us pray,' and we closed our eyes. When we opened them again, they had the land and we had the Bible. Maybe we got the better end of the deal."[15] Regardless of who got the better end of the deal, Archbishop Tutu preaches a God who loves people of all races and wants them all to enjoy a peace founded on justice.

In an address to students at the University of Natal, Archbishop Tutu described a time in England when he went to a party where for some reason the guests had to buy a cup of tea. When he offered to buy a cup for an acquaintance, the man replied, "No, I won't be subsidized."[16] The archbishop described the common attitude of wanting to pay one's own way, and then he explained that often people carry that attitude over to their relationship with God. They feel they have to prove themselves before God can love them; that leads to the kind of arrogance exhibited by the Pharisee praying at the front of the Temple. Only an openness to God's self-revelation in the scriptures and in human history, plus a willingness to admit one's own sinfulness, can help Christians avoid distorted images of God—and of themselves and other people.

Simone Weil (1909–43) reminds us that not everyone who grows in his or her images of God belongs to a religious denomination.[17] Though the family was of Jewish descent on both sides, the Weils of Paris simply considered themselves French. After her university studies in philosophy, Simone taught in several schools, worked with trade union leaders, and did factory work herself—always with fragile health. In 1938 she made a Holy Week retreat at the Benedictine monastery of Solesmes, an experience that marked a turning point in her relationship to God. In 1940, in order to escape the Nazis, she and her parents were forced to leave Paris for Marseilles, where Simone became a good friend of J.M. Perrin, a Dominican priest in that city. Two years later the Weil family arrived in New York, but within a few months Simone returned to England where she worked for the French provisional government, promoting her plan to send nurses to the front lines of the war. The following year she died of tuberculosis and malnutrition.

Simone Weil constantly emphasized God's respect for the freedom men and women enjoy in the divine plan for creation. God is all-powerful but chooses not to exercise that power everywhere. One of the obstacles to baptism for her was the ease with which people can identify temporal power with spiritual good—to the detriment of the latter. She once said to Father Perrin that she feared social organizations like the church because she felt herself too easily influenced. "I know that if at this moment I had before me a chorus of 20 young Germans singing Nazi songs, a part of my soul would instantly become Nazi. That is a great weakness, but that is how I am."[18] She felt that twentieth-century people wanted to escape all limits, including God, in the name of freedom and in this very process became more vulnerable to enslaving ideologies and mass movements. She believed that if people neglect the spiritual side of human nature and the resulting obligations, the social and political consequences will be disastrous.

Simone Weil's path to God came not only from her studies and involvement in current events. While on retreat at Solesmes she met an Oxford student, who introduced her to George Herbert and the seventeenth-century English metaphysical poets. Their religious insight helped her deal with her own physical sufferings and later the war in her homeland. She once wrote that nothing among human beings has such power to keep our gaze fixed ever more intensely on God than friendship for the friends of God.[19] The communion of saints was very real to her, playing a major role in her evolving images of God.

Our Own Prayer, Personal/Family Crises, and Images of God

Other people's prayers may help us see how a person grows in his or her images of God, but asking which images of God are growing or are being resisted in one's own prayer may be even more helpful. If in facing a personal or family crisis we find prayer a somewhat unsatisfactory ally, perhaps this represents a kind of "spiritual angina," a warning signal that calls for attention.

If my prayers presuppose that I need to catch God's attention and convince him that my case is different, that my case deserves his special intervention in order to resolve it as I think best, then I may well come away feeling unsatisfied when my father's cancer doesn't go into remission, my child's divorce becomes final, or the results of my neighbor's tests are not very encouraging. Prayer can become a way of saying "the ball is in your court, God" rather than admitting that, even as I pray, God is helping me to respond constructively to whatever causes me to pray.

Praying "harder"—in the sense of new prayers, longer prayers, promises of charitable deeds if the prayer is answered—never solves anything by itself because it tends to reinforce inadequate images of God. Of course, such prayer might show up a person's impoverished images of God and lead him or her to more truthful images.

If Ann prays that her husband Brad will admit his alcoholism and seek treatment, she may pray as though God had given Brad the affliction and now it's time to take it away. As she prays, she may blame herself for "driving him to drink." She may be tempted to accept too much responsibility for Brad's actions and not enough for her own. Prayer might lead her to constructive action, such as asking friends and family members to help her intervene to cut through the denial and cover-up. Or she might keep stating the problem wrongly— "Brad's alcoholism is God's way of punishing me because I . . . "—with the result that she comes to think of God as aloof and unconcerned about individuals and their problems.

Honest prayer is no quick fix; it represents a risky encounter with the living God and with our true selves. Honest prayer may well highlight our need to take action; for example, Brad's alcoholism is not God's will but a disease that can be kept under control. God's way of answering Ann's prayer may be by giving her courage to do what she had not intended to do when she began praying: intervene and refuse to continue as an enabler of Brad's disease. That might not seem like an answer to Ann's prayer because it looks as though God is not making any intervention, but perhaps that is how God respects human freedom.

Now let's suppose that Ann and Brad have a 15-year-old son, Kevin, who has his own problems. If Ann uses prayer as a way of avoiding her responsibilities, Kevin could very easily develop a twisted image of God. In fact, years later as an adult, he might still be dealing with the effect of his father's alcoholism on his own life.

Although Brad's alcoholism is not fundamentally a religious problem, Kevin's problem could have strong religious implications because of the twisted images of

God he links to his father's disease and his mother's approach to prayer. On the other hand, if prayer leads Ann to deal more constructively with Brad's alcoholism, and if Kevin realizes that, his images of God could grow in a healthy way.

Praying during a personal or family crisis is always worthwhile, but it should lead to greater honesty about what God can do and what God expects us to do regarding the situation. Even if events are completely beyond our control, as when I prayed for the lives of my prematurely born nephews, how we react to what finally happens and how we help others react to those events is, with the help of God's grace, very much under our control.

We think that a personal or family crisis means a single decision; for example, Ann decides to seek help in making an intervention about Brad's alcoholism. That may be the major decision in this case, but in making it Ann is also making a decision about the kind of person she will be, as opposed to the kind of person she has been. If Ann has a strong belief in God, what she decides to do about her husband's alcoholism is also a decision about the kind of God she worships. If previously she thought that Brad's alcoholism was God's way of punishing her for some failing on her part, and if she then decides to intervene, she will develop new images of God, stop believing in God altogether, or simply go through the motions of believing in God.

Nothing is ever the same after a personal or family crisis. If Brad admits his alcoholism, seeks treatment, and stops drinking, Ann may find the new Brad more difficult than the old Brad because his uncontrolled drinking had camouflaged other problems in their relationship. If Brad stops drinking, those other problems will remain, waiting for him and Ann to make the needed decisions.

Prayer may help both of them to grow in honesty with each other as they grow in honesty with God. Brad and Ann could well come to love one another more deeply than they had ever imagined was possible.

Developing New Images of God in Prayer

Whether we like it or not, prayer's natural tendency is to draw us away from comfortable images of God, ourselves, and others and lead us to larger images of God and more honest images of ourselves and others. If we find that our prayer is becoming routine and stale, it may indicate not that God is drawing away from us, but that we are afraid to move closer to him, afraid to move beyond our present images of God, ourselves, and others because we fear the demands that new images might make.

For example, if my image of God's will is that God has planned out my life in great detail (picked out my marriage partner or decided that I should be single, decided that I should be a computer programmer rather than a lion tamer, selected where I should live, and so on), that image of God turns my prayers of petition into requests that God put a few more of his cards on the table, so to speak. Such an image of God may be fairly satisfying as long as my life is going smoothly (I feel that God is revealing his plans, and I like what is happening), but if a crisis arises and my prayers don't seem to be answered, then I may lose motivation to pray. I may remember my previous prayers as consoling experiences and now my praying is anything but consoling.

Is it possible that I have confused my reasons for praying? Is it possible that now my seemingly useless prayer reflects the fact that I am in a kind of no-man's land spiritually? That, to use Matthew Arnold's phrase, I am "wandering between two worlds—the one dead, the other powerless to be born"? Arnold used that expression in "Stanzas From the Grand Chartreuse," his poem about the rational, scientific spirit of the nineteenth century, a spirit that seemed to have little use for the life of prayer and penance as practiced centuries before by the monks of the Grand Chartreuse.[20] Matthew Arnold admired his own historical era, but he felt something valuable had been lost from the era of the Grand Chartreuse monks.

Few people enjoy the feeling of wandering between two worlds. Yet if our prayer opens us up to the goodness of God, our own condition of being simultaneously graced and sinful, the fact that other people are also created in the image of God, in a certain sense we will always live between two worlds: the one where we know our own way around and the one where God wants to show us his way around. We will live between a world where we know what our decisions will cost us and a world where we fear that the right decisions may be too costly, that they may stretch us further than we want to be stretched.

If we pray honestly and with perseverance, our images of God must expand. For example, we will probably become more cautious in speaking about God's will. According to St. Paul, God's will is that we grow in holiness (see 1 Thes 4:3), but that does not indicate whether Brian Jones should become holy as a husband and father, as a priest or religious, or as a single person. That does not indicate whether Jennifer Smith should marry Fred or Alex or anyone at all, whether she should be a nurse, lawyer, or work full-time at home. Some choices are more reasonable than others; there is a certain calm and peacefulness about choices made in a spirit of openness to God's grace. But we should be slow to identify one particular choice as God's will, and we should be especially slow to use that expression when we console someone grieving over the death of a friend or relative, or over some other personal loss. Although we may not mean any harm, it can cause the person to feel persecuted by God. The three "comforters" who came to console Job would have given better comfort if they had not been so quick to speak of Job's sufferings as God's will. According to God's speech at the end of the book, only Job had spoken truthfully about God; Job was asked to offer sacrifice to expiate the sins of his "comforters."

In the case of Job's three friends, God's will was probably that they help Job express his anger and get on with life rather than trying to shame him into silence for feeling that God ought to answer a few questions about the kind of world he created, a world where the innocent often suffer. I think that part of the problem with Job's friends arose from their images of God, images reinforced by a persevering but perhaps not always honest prayer. At times they may have prayed as the Pharisee at the front of the Temple prayed.

Honest and persevering prayer should lead us to images of God we could not have appreciated earlier. For example, we often speak of God as a loving father. But if a child is abused by his or her father, what meaning can God as loving father have for that child? The child lacks a frame of reference to make any sense of that image of God. Similarly, how can a person understand the expression "God as just judge" if the only judges whom that person knows are not interested in justice but in perpetuating a totalitarian system?

In such cases the person may have to begin with another image and pray accordingly. It may take years before the child abused by his or her father can apply the expression "loving Father" to God. Honest and persevering prayer will lead to many images of God. Prayer enables the person to work out the initial difficulties connected with a new image; for example, if God is a loving father, why does he allow so much suffering?

Honest and persevering prayer praises God and leads to an integration of all aspects of our life. If God is not allowed to influence some part of our life, that indicates that our prayer has not been as honest and persevering as it needs to be.

The men who passed by the man half-dead on the road between Jerusalem and Jericho were probably very religious in many senses of the word, but their lives were not as integrated as that of the Samaritan. The elder brother in the parable of the prodigal son may have been a good person in some ways, but part of his life was apparently not open to God's grace. The elder brother and his father may have prayed side by side, but the father was probably more open to different images of God. That would partially explain their different reactions to the return of the prodigal son. The elder brother may have considered his images of God very orthodox. The Pharisees for whom Jesus told the parable certainly felt their images of God were orthodox, and Jesus disagreed.

If I feel a dryness in prayer, if I feel that my prayer is tending toward formalism without inner conviction, perhaps my images of God are too tidy, too domesticated, too non-threatening. Maybe I should ask, Is my image of God open to the breadth of the scriptures and the church's reflection on God's word? Am I protecting one image of God because others seem too risky? Am I avoiding other images of God that might change my relationship with God, my self-image, and my relations with others?

Prayer as an Element of Conversion and Start of Works of Charity

Although we may speak of prayer as something we do after we have converted, our conversion usually takes shape and solidifies as we praise God, ask pardon for ourselves, and seek some assistance for a friend or relative. Neither prayer nor conversion is ever finished.

In *When Bad Things Happen to Good People*, Rabbi Harold Kushner addresses the question of what good it does to pray for someone suffering when we know very well that the prayer may not succeed in the sense of assuring a cure, mending a broken heart, or addressing whatever need caused us to start praying in the first place. He answers that such prayers are valuable because they can help us see ourselves and the suffering person in a new light. Despite our inability to guarantee that the person's suffering will be relieved as we think best, in prayer we often see that we have a great deal of freedom in choosing how we will deal with that person's suffering. In prayer we may receive the insight and encouragement to help that person see that

> illnesses, accidents, human tragedies kill people. But they do not necessarily kill life or faith. If the death and suffering of someone we love makes us bitter, jealous, against all religion, and incapable of happiness, we turn the person who died into one of the "devil's martyrs" [witnesses against God].[21]

Prayer does not guarantee conversion because a person can always pray as Javert did or as the Pharisee in the Temple did, in a way that reinforces self-serving images of God, oneself, and others. Honest, persevering prayer, however, inevitably leads to conversion; to seeing God, oneself, and others from a wider perspective; and then to works of charity.

I fear that the woman who wrote to me saying, "God answered my prayers better when I bothered him less," may have unintentionally set herself on the path where totally honest prayer and radical conversion become increasingly difficult. A prayer that does not lead to the result we wanted should not lead to bitterness toward God or anyone else. If it does, the prayer was fundamentally flawed.

Honest, persevering prayer should lead us to works of charity and to works of justice that recognize the God-given dignity of people we might easily ignore. How had the good Samaritan prayed before he encountered that man left half-dead on the road between Jerusalem and Jericho? The good Samaritan's action proceeds from prayer and should lead to prayer, but this does not mean that the Samaritan's conversion is assured. Conversion is never irreversible, and for that reason each moment we live and each person we meet is important. Not every decision I make may be major, but none of them is insignificant in the eyes of God. Perhaps the priest and the Levite on that same road were saving their energies and their charity for more important, more public cases. If so, their works of charity would simply reinforce the same kind of smugness Mrs. Turpin displayed in the doctor's waiting room.

In the last judgment parable the saved and the condemned have quite different images of God, self, and others. One group reinforces its conversion and solidifies its images through works of compassion. The other group solidifies those same images through acts of smugness, by congratulating themselves on the least little sacrifice and by always seeing the other person as an object and not as someone created and loved by God. The *Catholic Worker* woodcut that shows Christ standing in a bread line powerfully echoes Jesus' message.

Honest, persevering prayer inevitably leads us back to the scriptures, to the parts we have overlooked or misinterpreted as we resisted conversion in relation to our images of God, self, and others. The next chapter will show how and at what cost we must continue growing with the scriptures.

For Personal Reflection

1. Have I ever prayed to change God's mind and been disappointed? How did that experience affect my images of God?
2. In my prayer, is God really the fixed point? Or am I? What difference does that make? On what images of God is my prayer usually based?
3. Is honest prayer ever untidy and messy? Have I ever prayed as Job did but doubted that I was praying at all? Can prayers said in anger be real prayers?
4. Have I ever had a "perfect joy" experience such as Francis of Assisi described? Did it affect the way I prayed?
5. Have I ever said "I'll pray for you" as a way of putting distance between myself and someone in physical or spiritual pain? Shouldn't prayer reduce the distance and lead to works of charity?
6. Has my prayer ever been a "wandering between two worlds, the one dead, the other powerless to be born"? Is that necessarily a bad thing? How did I—or am I—handling that situation?

For Group Discussion

1. The Pharisee praying in the Temple thanked God that he was not like the tax collector. How might a modern-day Pharisee express that same attitude in prayer?
2. Prayer can challenge a false image of God, of oneself, and of others—or it can reaffirm those false images. What makes the difference?
3. Dorothy Day once said, "Don't call me a saint. I don't want to be dismissed so easily." Why are we so tempted to think that the saints never had interior struggles with their images of God, themselves, and their neighbors?
4. Is my admiration for any holy person related to that person's growth in prayer? Who? What was the growth?
5. Prayer's natural tendency is to draw us away from cozy images of God, ourselves, and others and lead us to more

authentic images of God, ourselves, and others. Is that true?
If so, does that mean that group prayer must eventually
challenge our cozy images?

6. What happens if people make their religion too private,
always preferring private prayer to public prayer? Did the
elder son in the prodigal son story perhaps have an overly
private sense of religion?

Further Resources

Mary Collins, *Women at Prayer* (Mahwah, NJ: Paulist Press,
1987).

Dorothy Day, *Meditations*, comp. Stanley Vishnewski (Mahwah, NJ: Paulist Press, 1970).

Eric Doyle, O.F.M., *Saint Francis and the Song of the Brotherhood*
(New York: Harper and Row, 1981).

Meister Eckhart, *Teacher and Preacher* (Mahwah, NJ: Paulist
Press, 1986). This volume on Eckhart's biblical commentaries, Latin sermons, and German sermons includes a
sixteen-page article entitled "Meister Eckhart on Speaking About God."

Meister Eckhart, *The Essential Sermons, Commentaries, Treatises,
and Defense* (Mahwah, NJ: Paulist Press, 1981).

Greg Friedman, O.F.M., *It Begins With Friendship: A Fresh Approach to Prayer* (Cincinnati, OH: St. Anthony Messenger
Press, 1984).

Virginia Froehle, R.S.M., *In Her Presence: Prayer Experiences Exploring Feminine Images of God*, audiocassete (Cincinnati,
OH: St. Anthony Messenger Press, 1986).

Thomas Green, S.J., *Darkness in the Marketplace* (Notre Dame,
IN: Ave Maria Press, 1981).

Gloria Hutchinson, *Christ Encounters: A Journal Retreat* (Notre
Dame, IN: Ave Maria Press, 1988).

Joachim Jeremias, *The Prayers of Jesus* (Philadelphia,
PA: Fortress Press, 1977). In prayer, especially in times of
stress, Jesus clarified what it meant to be Messiah. Prayer
helps his followers to learn the meaning of discipleship.

Julian of Norwich, *Showings* (Mahwah, NJ: Paulist Press, 1978).
Mystics are often controversial people because they use

unconventional language about God, and this leads to questions about their orthodoxy.

Eloi Leclerc, O.F.M., *Song of the Dawn* (Chicago: Franciscan Herald Press, 1977).

Jean-Marie Lustiger, *First Steps in Prayer* (Staten Island, NY: Alba House, 1987).

Rea McDonnell, S.S.N.D., and Rachel Callahan, C.S.C., *Hope for Healing: Good News for Adult Children of Alcoholics* (Mahwah, NJ: Paulist Press, 1987).

Miriam Pollard, O.C.S.O., *The Laughter of God: At Ease with Prayer* (Wilmington, DE: Michael Glazier, Inc., 1986).

Joyce Rupp, O.S.M., *Praying Our Goodbyes* (Notre Dame, IN: Ave Maria Press, 1988).

Susan Saint Sing, *Living With Sickness: A Struggle Toward Meaning* (Cincinnati, OH: St. Anthony Messenger Press, 1987).

Jean Vanier, *Man and Woman He Made Them* (Mahwah, NJ: Paulist Press, 1985).

Jean Vanier, *The Broken Body: Journey to Wholeness* (Mahwah, NJ: Paulist Press, 1988).

SIX

Growing With the Scriptures

According to a children's story, one day four blind men encountered an elephant but did not know what it was. "It's like a log," said one who had flung his arms around the elephant's leg. "No! It is like a rope," said another who had caught hold of its tail. "It is more like a fan," said the third. He was feeling the shape of the elephant's ear. "It is something with no beginning and no end," said the fourth who was walking round and round the animal, feeling its sides.[1]

We cannot touch God the way those blind men felt the elephant, of course, but often our descriptions of God are no more accurate than the blind men's description of the elephant. This is especially true if our images of God are based on very sketchy knowledge of the most direct source of God's self-revelation, the scriptures. If someone knew only the Book of Joshua, for example, he or she might be tempted to think that God is very bloodthirsty. Acquainted only with the Book of Proverbs, another person might think that God hands out or withholds riches on the basis of the person's individual holiness. A third person, who knew only the parables of the prodigal son and the good shepherd, could be tempted to think that God is so forgiving that eternal damnation is impossible. And what kind of an image would someone have who read only the Book of Revelation? Even the greatest theologians and biblical scholars do not claim to have a completely adequate understanding of God.

Most of us prefer to make things as uncomplicated as possible. Thus we are constantly tempted to sum up God's self-revelation in a single image or in a catchy slogan. Although we may like to think of ourselves as realists, we often find dealing with reality rather confusing and thus tend to overlook or downgrade troublesome passages or images of God.

Problems in the Second Century

The Roman priest Marcion was a very early example of this tendency to oversimplify. How can you reconcile the God of the conquest of Canaan, the God of the Mosaic Law, with the Father, Son, and Holy Spirit presented in the New Testament? Hasn't the New Testament liberated us from the dead legalism of the Old? Wasn't the Old Testament's God of wrath and justice replaced by the New Testament's God of mercy and love?

Marcion decided that the differences between the Hebrew scriptures and the Christian scriptures required a belief in two quite different gods, with the New Testament God winning out. For Marcion, this was the meaning of Paul's statement that if anyone is in Christ that person is a new creation. Now that Jesus has come, said Marcion, there is no need to read the Hebrew scriptures; they have been superseded by the Christian scriptures.

In the mid-second century the church declared Marcion's teaching heretical and affirmed that there is only one God, who is the originator and inspirer of both testaments. Although Marcion's error was formally condemned long ago, his idea that the New Testament presents a gracious, loving God opposed to the strict, legalistic God of the Hebrew scriptures lives on.

In a further effort to make life more simple, Marcion accepted as divinely inspired only the gospel of Luke and ten letters attributed to St. Paul. In order to explain its faith and to guard against future selective reading of the scriptures, the church eventually had to make an official decision about which books, in fact, belong to the New Testament. In 393 a provincial council of Carthage affirmed the New Testament canon as we know it, but only in 1546 did a general council (Trent) give formal approval to a list that had been accepted without major challenge for over one thousand years.

For the Hebrew scriptures the church simply accepted the Greek canon, which had existed before the time of Christ. After the time of Christ, some rabbis felt that only those works written in Hebrew should be considered inspired, and so they drew up a Hebrew canon, which does not include Wisdom, Sirach, Maccabees, Tobit, Judith, and Baruch, plus parts of Daniel and Esther.

The New Testament is the church's book. That does not mean that the church is above scripture, but it does mean that the New Testament cannot be fully understood apart from the faith community for which these individual writings were intended, or apart from the larger faith community that recognized these books as inspired and continues to read and ponder their teaching. This is the dynamic meaning of the term *Tradition*, which for Roman Catholics is not an alternative source of God's revelation but rather an integral part of God's self-revelation in the scriptures.

Saying that the New Testament is the church's book does not mean that its vocabulary and literary genres cannot or should not be studied in a serious and scientific way. Indeed, a non-Christian expert in ancient languages, history, or literary genres can make important contributions to our understanding of scriptural texts, but unless that person is an active Christian believer, the New Testament remains, in some ways, a closed book.

Similarly, the Hebrew scriptures did not fall from heaven neatly printed, bound, and titled *God's Self-Revelation*. The Hebrew scriptures represent a two thousand-year journey in faith with an extremely valuable reflection on the origin of the world and on God's respect for human freedom, which made sin possible. I believe that God intended the Hebrew scriptures and the New Testament to be read together.

The Church's Caution About Simplistic Thinking

Some people have suggested that Marcion's ideas were condemned because they were anti-Jewish. Actually, Marcion considered his teaching orthodox and hoped that his explanation of the scriptures would lead Jewish believers to Christianity.[2] The church disagreed and condemned Marcion's position. Unfortunately, his error lives on, especially where anti-Semitism seeks to make itself respectable by using Christianity as an acceptable veneer. Marcion's mistake, however, concerned not only the relation of the Hebrew scriptures and the New Testament but also the way we speak about God and the limits of human language in that attempt. According to scripture scholar Robert Murray, Marcion

> saw conflicting statements about God and his dealings with humans, found these antitheses intolerable, and decided that the only solution was the one which he found logical: two Gods and two dispensations, the first God, his creation and revelation being totally inferior to, and totally superseded by, the God newly revealed in Christ and his dispensation of Grace.[3]

Murray further says that even though Marcion's main idea was rejected by the church, the error of 'monolithic' thinking was not shown up, and the scandal of the different faces of God in the Old Testament, and between the Old and the New, was not explained clearly enough as what it really is—no scandal, but an invitation to appreciate the marvelous theological stimulus God has given us wherever we recognize diversity in the biblical presentations of God—and that is primarily in the Old Testament.[4]

The scriptures speak about God in many ways, including ways that can seem contradictory. Such pluralism of "God-talk" may be jarring or upsetting to someone who wants just the facts. Such a person may be very tempted to go back to the fundamentals, which, in practice, usually means trimming theological pluralism—like an overgrown hedge—so that a simpler, more manageable God emerges. Pope John Paul II once told a group of United States bishops that the church recognizes and fosters a legitimate pluralism in theology. He quoted Pope Paul VI, who said that "a moderate diversity of opinions is compatible with the unity of the faith and with fidelity towards the teachings and norms of the magisterium."[5] A legitimate pluralism in theology flows from the scriptures, which contain quite diverse images of God.

Of course, everything that calls itself theological pluralism isn't necessarily that. The faith community may have to declare that certain ideas are not part of its faith; for example, that Jesus was not God but only a good man, or that when Jesus said "This is my body" he was speaking poetically. But the need to articulate its faith more clearly does not mean that the church can afford to think simplistically. However attractive such thinking might appear—and it is always clear and decisive—it carries a hidden but very high price. Robert Murray says that accepting the canon of the scriptures as God's gift to us

binds us not only to the whole and the parts,
but also to its pluriformity and its paradoxes.
These are so great that Christians are challenged
to approach the Bible not only with the 'obedience of faith' but also with readiness to stretch
our minds, with intelligently informed imagination, and to learn to think dialectically as well as
in one straight line. Different parts of the canon
may ask us quite different questions and hint at
different answers; God's word to us is not only
what each book or passage says, but also both
the dialectic and the invitation to form conclusions from the diversity.[6]

A church that accepts four gospels as inspired (and they
clearly do not agree in all details no matter what gym-
nastics a person may perform on the texts) and that reads
two quite different creation accounts in the Book of Genesis is a church that knows the need for orthodoxy does
not eliminate the need for different images and ways of
talking about God.

Economic monopolies are efficient only for the few
who control the monopolies, not for the many who need
their services. A theological monopoly has the same inherent danger and in time will necessarily lack the ideas
and vocabulary to deal with challenges to the individual's and the church's faith. For this reason Christianity encourages "both/and" thinking; it uses "either/or"
thinking rather sparingly, only on crucial issues (Was
Jesus truly God? Do the Hebrew scriptures and New
Testament reveal a different God?). Even if some individuals or groups within Christianity prefer and pride
themselves on "either/or" thinking, such an approach
does not reflect Christianity's deepest roots—much less
the deepest roots of Old Testament "God-talk."[7]

Much anguish and bloodshed might have been avoided if all Christians respected the need for theological pluralism half as much as they endorsed the need to declare some ideas heretical. During the Reformation the question for some people was whether a person is saved by faith or by good works. Is God's self-revelation given through scripture alone or does Tradition have a role? The language of polemics, whether from the Lutheran side or the Catholic side, may seem forceful and exciting, but such language rarely favors discovering the whole truth of God's revelation. Catholics could point to the Letter of James, which says that faith without works is dead; Luther and his followers could point to the Letter to the Romans, which quotes Habakkuk "the just man lives by faith." But who was quoting the Letter to the Galatians, which says that what matters is "faith which works through love" (Gal 5:6)?

Catholic polemicists could use a certain notion of Tradition to foster a theological monopoly and thus forestall the need for reform in theology and church practice. Lutheran polemicists could blast the Letter of James as an "epistle of straw" and speak of a "canon within the canon," which would give their reading of the Letter to the Romans more weight because Paul was a more influential New Testament writer than James. Anyone who would say that polemicists on each side had misread the scriptures (and Tradition) would quickly be labelled wishy-washy and a secret agent for the other side. Simplistic thinking has its short-term rewards, but twentieth-century Christians are still paying the price for the sixteenth-century brand of such thinking.

The Galileo case in the seventeenth century was seen by some Christians as an attack on religion rather than an attempt to understand better the universe in which we live, the universe God created. Those Christians felt that silencing Galileo was the only way to protect the scriptures from scientific, rationalist challenges. Today most Christians can say that the author of the Book of Joshua was using the inaccurate science of his day when he said that Joshua ordered the sun to stand still. Biblical inspiration does not guarantee scientific accuracy.

During the Age of Enlightenment some Christians in the West felt that the church gave too little respect to reason and to new scientific developments in the world. For them, being progressive meant leaving behind a tradition-bound and scripturally gullible church in favor of reason, a view of God as the master craftsman of the universe, and an openness to new political arrangements. During the Enlightenment some Christians considered the institutional church a betrayal of Christianity; they felt that our God-given dignity and freedom could be promoted only by honoring certain humanitarian ideals in the scriptures while keeping the painfully human church at arm's length. This approach to God and religion eventually received the name Deism and was the dominant religious perspective of thinkers such as John Locke, Benjamin Franklin, and Thomas Jefferson.

Deism tends to see God as the creator of the universe, the master craftsman, the giant clock maker, who sets the world in motion and then effectively goes off, leaving it to its own devices. A person can become free, said the Deists, only if God becomes more remote, less directly involved in daily life. Deism bears some resemblance to classical Stoicism with its emphasis on reason, suspicion of emotion, and esteem for "nature's law."[8]

During the Age of Enlightenment some Christians began to question if the Genesis accounts of creation were literally true, if Moses indeed wrote the entire Pentateuch and if the miracles of Jesus recorded in the gospels were truly miracles or had some natural explanation. At this time students of the scriptures began to speak of different literary/theological traditions in the Book of Genesis. People began to wonder if the first eleven chapters of Genesis, the creation to Abraham, were literal history.

With these new questions, many Christians felt very threatened. Suddenly, *rationalist* became a nasty word when applied to a Christian, and faith and science were seen by some Christians as irreconcilable adversaries. When Charles Darwin proposed the theory of evolution in the nineteenth century, some Christians turned "godless science" into a single thought, even if it remained two words. Again, anyone who counselled both/and thinking instead of either/or thinking about the Book of Genesis and the theory of evolution was regarded with suspicion from both sides. Christian churches are still living with the difficulties created by the divorce of religion and modern science.

Critics of the Deist approach say that the Deists underestimated original sin and too confidently believed in the perfectibility of the human person. Without intending to do so, Deism can drift into a practical, even if unacknowledged, atheism in which God's influence becomes remote and the laws of nature explain all life's mysteries.

Deism can lead to a civic religion capable of being manipulated for any number of non-religious purposes. Adherents of such a civic religion can even become indignant when they feel that religious leaders are becoming too political.

Does God work directly in the world or did he create a giant machine and then turn it over to human

beings? Deists tend to the latter idea while suspecting
that those who favor the former one are superstitious.
More traditional Christians can easily label Deist concerns about human freedom and dignity as secularism
or modernism and thus refuse to take those concerns
seriously. Though that strategy may seem decisive, it
simply guarantees that the Deist questions will remain
very powerful.

Scripture scholar Eugene Maly once lectured on the
three main ways that people picture God's action in the
world.[9] He said that the inclusivist world view sees a
transcendent God and secular reality as having a direct
and ongoing relationship. Thus God sends earthquakes,
thunderstorms, prosperity, and destitution to reward or
punish individuals and groups. For some people this
is the sum total of what the Bible teaches. According
to Maly, the correlative world view sees a temporary
relationship of God with the world; here God is not
always directly at work in human history. Such a viewpoint can easily give way to the exclusivist world view
(agnosticism or atheism) where God has no role in the
world.

Maly said that the biblical writers presumed the
inclusivist world view; so did ancient pagan writers.
Ongoing history revealed God to the ancient Hebrews;
divinity was not exhausted in God's continuing mani-
festation of himself. During the medieval period some
Christians began to think of God as touching the natural order in sacraments, miracles, and gifts of the Spirit.
This approach was intended to recognize a certain auton-
omy in nature and to affirm God's freedom in revelation.
Many Christians today have this correlative world view.
Modern society tends to favor the exclusivist viewpoint,
a God who recedes in importance as technology and
science advance. The inclusivist viewpoint, modified by

a more biblical understanding of God's will, seems the only viable approach.

Maly said that for the Old Testament writers God's spirit is always present, but more intense at certain times. God acts always and everywhere through the spirit. The exclusivist viewpoint leads to a situation where life is bleak and chaotic, and society has no central organizing principle. God is not on the outside waiting to be invited in, said Maly, but rather is constantly moving us to transform ourselves in his power.

Theologian Frederick Sontag addresses similar concerns in *The God of Evil: An Argument From the Existence of the Devil.* He investigates modern atheism and concludes that it stems, in part, from the refusal by some Christians to take evil seriously, by their tendency to give simplistic answers to serious questions. Sontag says:

> The simpler a God is to find, the easier he is to reject. The harder he is to find, the more difficult he is to reject definitively, but the concept is also more difficult for us to confirm and maintain belief in.[10]

Sontag explains that simple answers are attractive but lack holding power, which comes only from plunging beneath the surface. If evil did not require an accounting, we would have stopped being concerned with it long ago or would have accepted a surface explanation. Sontag observes:

> Our views of God vary; they blend into one another. . . . The only proper reply to any announcement of the death of God is: "Which God?" It would seem impossible to prove that a being corresponding to each of all the possible concepts of God could in fact not exist, since you would have to examine an infinite number in order to do this. It is a perfectly natural and

healthy phenomenon for some one concept of God to "die," and it also tells us a great deal about our relationship to God.[11]

Simplistic religious answers to serious questions carry their own seeds of destruction. Sontag says that theism tends to atheism when what God accomplishes can also be accomplished without him. I believe Maly was making the same point. Unless God takes decisive action in the face of evil, he will soon be seen as superfluous. Remaining in theism, says Sontag, takes constant effort because any philosophical concept of God tends to fade under new conditions; unless people make a constant effort, they tend to drift into atheism, explicit or practical. But then do those who abandon theism because of their dissatisfaction with its answer to the question of evil find a better answer in atheism?

Anti-Semitism: Perversion of the Biblical Revelation

Much as Christians like to think of themselves as having biblical images of God, they often settle for caricatures of the biblical revelation. Perhaps nowhere is this more evident than in attempts to give theological respectability to anti-Semitism. Here God is seen as offering friendship to the Jewish people and later rejecting them forever for not accepting Jesus Christ as Messiah and for the part some Jews played in the death of Jesus. Such a reading of the New Testament tends to emphasize texts like "Let his blood be on us and on our children" (Mt 27:25) and to see Pilate as the innocent victim in a political power play.

Anti-Semitism in Christian trappings will not spend much, if any, time on Paul's Letter to the Romans, where he addresses a Jewish Christian audience on the relation of Judaism and Christianity. Here Paul specifically rules out the idea that God has withdrawn his election of the

Jewish people. When Paul asks if it is possible that God abandoned his people, he answers, "Out of the question! . . . God never abandoned his people to whom, ages ago, he had given recognition" (Rom 11:1–2).

A "Christian anti-Semitism" will also spend little time reflecting on the Second Vatican Council's statement about Jews and the death of Jesus:

> True, authorities of the Jews and those who followed their lead pressed for the death of Christ (cf. Jn 19:6); still, what happened in His passion cannot be blamed upon all the Jews then living, without distinction, nor upon the Jews of today. Although the Church is the new people of God, the Jews should not be presented as repudiated or cursed by God, as if such views followed from the Holy Scriptures. All should take pains, then, lest in catechetical instruction and in the preaching of God's Word they teach anything out of harmony with the truth of the gospel and the spirit of Christ.[12]

If that official statement had been made and lived out centuries earlier, Christian/Jewish relations today would probably be more faithful to the entire teaching of the New Testament.

Life for European Jews in the Middles Ages—in the countries where they had not been expelled—became more dangerous during Holy Week, when, on hearing the gospel accounts, some Christians decided to avenge Christ's death. Nor have preachers always accurately presented the church's faith on this subject. Some Christians undoubtedly thought they were carrying out God's will when they persecuted the Jews.

Every ten years the passion play in Oberammergau, West Germany attracts worldwide attention and charges that the play is anti-Semitic; the same question surfaces about less famous passion plays and the way in which the passion accounts should be presented and preached about during Holy Week. In 1988 the National Conference of Catholic Bishops' Committee for Ecumenical and Interreligious Affairs issued a document that addressed these concerns. "Any presentations which explicitly or implicitly seek to shift responsibility from human sin onto this or that historical group, such as the Jews, can only be said to obscure a core Gospel truth."[13]

Recognizing that dramatic presentations favor sharp contrasts between characters, the document says that Jesus must not be depicted as opposed to the Mosaic Law. The Old Testament

> and the Jewish tradition founded on it must not be set against the New Testament in such a way that the former seems to constitute a religion of only justice, fear and legalism, with no appeal to the love of God and neighbor.[14]

Jews should not be portrayed as avaricious, bloodthirsty, or implacable enemies of Christ; crowd scenes should reflect the fact that "some in the crowd and among the Jewish leaders (e.g., Nicodemus, Joseph) supported Jesus and that the rest were manipulated by his opponents."[15]

> In sum, Judaism and Jewish society in the time of Christ and the apostles were complex realities, embracing many different trends, many spiritual, religious, social, and cultural values. Presentations of the passion should strive to reflect this spiritual vitality, avoiding any implication that Jesus' death was the result of religious antagonism between a stereotyped 'Judaism' and Christian doctrine.[16]

Passion plays rarely follow a single gospel account but rather tend to pick scenes and phrases from all four accounts. According to these guidelines, "To attempt to utilize the four passion narratives literally by picking one passage from one Gospel and the next from another Gospel, etc., is to risk violating the integrity of the texts themselves."[17] Ironically, a highly selective reading of biblical texts can encourage an unbiblical interpretation of the passion, death, and resurrection of Jesus.

The Bible as the Church's Book

The case of Marcion, many Lutheran and Catholic polemics during the Reformation, the Deism of the eighteenth century, and any "Bible-based" anti-Semitism of the last twenty centuries—all these cases illustrate what can happen when people seek a "biblical" God by reading the Bible very selectively and ignoring the church's prayerful interpretation of those same texts and the rest of the Bible. When Christians read the Bible, they need to remember not only that God inspired it but also that God counted on the church to recognize that inspiration. The Bible is the word of God, but it is also the church's book. A person's images of God cannot be truly biblical simply by reading selected biblical texts; those images of God must be open to the church's prayerful understanding of all the biblical texts, not simply the ones that favor the image of God a person may like best. Although an individual Christian may feel that his or her perception of God is thoroughly biblical, the person cannot avoid acknowledging the church's role in the interpretation of the scriptures. The person must be ready to complement one biblically-based image with other biblical images.

Without the Christian community, who can say whether Marcion presented the scriptures fairly or distorted them? Who can say whether the Deist presents a biblical God or an unbiblically aloof God? Who can say whether the New Testament justifies, or even commands, anti-Semitism?

In each case the adherents of these views have claimed that they were thinking and acting in an orthodox manner. Orthodoxy is important. Marcion, the Deists, and those who claim New Testament support for anti-Semitism are not quibbling over esoteric or peripheral matters. In some situations we need either/or thinking; in other situations we need both/and thinking. The difficulty with the groups listed above, and similar ones, is that they apply either/or thinking in the wrong situation.

The Christian community helps us to apply each kind of thinking to the appropriate situation. It often fosters both/and thinking where either/or thinking would be easier (for example, Jesus Christ is both God and man rather than merely God or merely man). And yet this same community sometimes declares that fidelity to the scriptures requires either/or thinking (for example, the church cannot accept Marcion's view of the Hebrew scriptures). Members of the Christian community cannot afford to cry heresy every time they hear something to which they are unaccustomed, but neither can they pretend that every theological disagreement is a quibble over words on a matter of secondary importance. A premature orthodoxy fights the wrong opponent in the wrong place; a dogmatic refusal to make any judgment about orthodoxy assumes that God's self-revelation can never be misunderstood in a serious way.

Judaism and Christianity do not believe that the entire world was created by a good God because this is easier than dualism. Rather, both religions believe that the Book of Genesis contains God's self-revelation on this important question.

Believing in determinism, that human freedom is an illusion, takes less effort than believing that the God who gave us freedom and intelligence expects us to use both wisely. Very often either/or thinking represents the path of least resistance whereas both/and thinking reflects a willingness to deal with a complex issue, even if that means accepting more personal responsibility for it.

Either/or thinking has the advantage of being quicker, but rapid movement into a false dichotomy (faith *vs.* good works or religion *vs.* science) can hardly be called progress. Both/and thinking is slower; it is usually a group enterprise and those who engage in such thinking may have to listen and reflect more.

We tend to underestimate the diversity in the Hebrew scriptures and in the New Testament. Of course, once we start to notice that diversity, we can miss the underlying unity of these inspired writings. For scriptural diversity and unity to be respected we need a community that is prayerfully reflecting on God's self-revelation and its application to the concrete situation in which that community lives. How can Christians wrestle with the "hard sayings" of the gospels unless there is a community committed to the entire scripture, even those parts that may require further prayer and study to be understood and put into practice? A case study may help illustrate this point.

In *The Churches the Apostles Left Behind*, scripture scholar Raymond Brown investigates how seven churches, with different strengths and weaknesses, survived the death of the apostles who founded them.[18] In a later book, *Biblical Exegesis and Church Doctrine*,[19] he studies those seven plus another church addressed by the Letter of James. Brown identifies three distinct churches within the Pauline tradition, and two more within the Johannine tradition. He further describes four distinct traditions within those churches, whose members were originally either Jewish or Gentile. The New Testament writings contain more diversity than we

realize. Anyone who reads Acts, chapter 15, and sup-
poses that the issue of Jewish/Gentile relations was settled definitively by the apostles at a Jerusalem council
around A.D. 49 must ignore a good deal of New Testament evidence.

God's self-revelation in the scriptures is not quite as
transparent as some Christians have believed; the "fundamentals" of the New Testament are not all that simple.
God may reveal himself privately to individuals apart
from the New Testament, but only the New Testament
revelation can be considered normative for all Christians.
Those scriptures, however, require a church to recognize
them as the word of God.

Fundamentalist Christians often see Tradition as an
attempt to water down or distort the word of God, but
unless they allow the Christian community some ongoing role in the prayerful interpretation of the scriptures,
why should we trust the church in telling us what the
canon of scriptures is? How can people who distrust all
notions of Tradition regarding the scriptures respond if
someone says that the New Testament includes writings
not inspired by God—or that the New Testament fails to
include writings God inspired for the sake of the whole
church? Like it or not, accepting the New Testament
means accepting the universal church, which continues
to recognize these writings as the word of God.

Only the universal church can mediate between different traditions within the scriptures. Only the universal
church can eventually decide when non-biblical language may be necessary in order to safeguard the biblical revelation. The first clear example of such a
decision came at the Council of Nicea (325). The bishops adopted a profession of faith that described Jesus as
homoousios ("of the same substance") in relation to God
the Father. This non-biblical term was needed to answer

the urgent question posed by Arius: Was Jesus truly God? The profession of faith commonly called the Nicene Creed (prayed in many churches on Sundays) is really the Nicene-Constantinopolitan Creed because in 381 another ecumenical council amended the earlier text to include a longer section on the Holy Spirit and belief in the church, baptism, the resurrection of the dead, and eternal life.

Only the universal church can decide if the Bible is invalidated when science shows that we live in a sun-centered universe rather than the earth-centered one presupposed in the Bible. Only the universal church can decide whether fidelity to the scriptures requires Christians to reject the theory of evolution. And that universal church may not be able to answer those questions adequately the first time they are asked. The initial church reaction to both Galileo's and Darwin's ideas was to reject them. In the time of Arius the bishops needed to meet and discuss the issue before they could declare the church's faith on the matter.

A church committed to the Hebrew scriptures and to the New Testament cannot afford to suppress or declare as allegories sayings or passages believers may find difficult. A church that recognizes that the scriptures are normative for the Christian faith cannot abdicate its responsibility to study and pray over this word of God and to describe its faith in non-biblical language if necessary (as at the Council of Nicea).

The church articulates its faith in many ways. Roman Catholics believe that bishops in union with the pope help to guarantee the apostolic character of the church. For this reason the bishops sometimes meet in ecumenical councils to decide doctrinal and disciplinary matters of major importance for the life of the church. Although several Christian churches see their apostolic character as partially preserved by the office of bishop, other Christian groups that do not have bishops consider themselves no less apostolic.

Since Roman Catholics recognize only twenty-one ecumenical councils since the time of Christ, one must admit that the bishops have other ways of helping to assure the church's apostolicity. They meet in regional groups, pray among themselves and with their local churches, encourage one another through visits and letters, and maintain their unity with the bishop of Rome. Maintaining that essential unity has taken different forms over the centuries. For example, once it was enough for priests to elect a new bishop or for bishops in a region to elect a new bishop and then inform the pope. Now the pope appoints new bishops.

If the Catholic church articulates its faith authoritatively through the ministry of bishops united in faith and charity with Peter's successor (the bishop of Rome), that same church also needs its theologians, saints, and mystics to help it remain faithful to the scriptures and to the church's Tradition. Theologians such as Athanasius, Augustine, Thomas Aquinas, Teresa of Avila, and John Courtney Murray, for example, have sought to respond to new and urgent questions raised in various generations. They have developed theological terms and concepts, often using non-biblical language but always in harmony with God's self-revelation as contained in the scriptures. Although all the theologians cited above experienced some opposition from their contemporaries, their teachings were eventually accepted by the church— not as the last word in theology but as useful for articulating the church's faith regarding the questions they investigated. Each of them represented a form of theological pluralism that the church eventually found useful and indeed necessary.

Saints, martyrs, and mystics such as Mary and Martha, Martin of Tours, Benedict, Julian of Norwich, Clare of Assisi, Catherine of Siena, Thomas More, Vincent de Paul, Elizabeth Ann Seton, and Kateri Tekakwitha have prayerfully witnessed to God's love for all people and our need to reflect that love in word and deed. In every age holy women and men have resisted attempts to oversimplify the gospel; they have given a contemporary face to the story of Martha and Mary, the story of the good Samaritan, and the Sermon on the Mount.

Other Christian groups may not formally beatify or canonize holy men and women, but they remember with respect those who have lived the gospel wholeheartedly. No one saintly person can possibly offer the church the wide variety of gospel-based witness it needs; each person does what is possible for him or her. God's grace and human freedom results in lives that inspire faith and build up the church of God. The lives of holy men and women are one part of the church's prayerful Tradition, which helps us understand the scriptures.

Who Determines the Church's Tradition?

The sad case of Archbishop Marcel Lefebvre illustrates what can happen when someone sets himself up as the only reliable interpreter of the church's Tradition. Unhappy with several Vatican II documents that he claimed betrayed the church's faith (especially the *Declaration on Religious Liberty*), Lefebvre established a religious community known as the Priestly Fraternity of St. Pius X. His seminary in Econe, Switzerland, trained priests for groups of Catholics who held similar views. The Tridentine Mass (a rite established by the Roman Missal of 1570 after the Council of Trent) became a touchstone of orthodoxy when Lefebvre and his followers refused to accept the New Order of the Mass approved by

Pope Paul VI in 1970. Lefebvre described the Tridentine Mass as "the Mass of the Church, the Mass of tradition, the Mass of all time."[20] In June 1976 Lefebvre ordained a group of priests against the express command of Paul VI and was suspended by the pope. Lefebvre continued to ordain priests who recognized only his authority and not that of the bishop in whose territory they ministered to "traditionalist" Catholics.

After a September 1976 meeting between Lefebvre and Pope Paul VI did not lead to any realistic hope for a reconciliation, the pope sent Lefebvre a letter which said, in part:

> In practice, you are claiming that you alone are the judge of what tradition embraces. . . . The concept of tradition that you invoke is distorted. Tradition is not a rigid and dead notion, a fact of a certain static sort which at a given moment of history blocks the life of this active organism which is the Church. . . . Tradition is inseparable from the living magisterium of the Church, just as it is inseparable from sacred Scripture.[21]

When Paul VI died in 1978 Lefebvre and his followers were as adamant as ever in rejecting what they regarded as the abuses springing from Vatican II and the heresy contained in some of its decrees.

In 1987 Archbishop Lefebvre and Cardinal Ratzinger held a number of meetings, which led Pope John Paul II to appoint Cardinal Edouard Gagnon to conduct an apostolic visitation of the Priestly Fraternity of St. Pius X with a hope of regularizing its relation—and Lefebvre's—to the church. After the visitation was completed but before any further steps were taken toward reconciliation, the pope addressed a public letter to Cardinal Ratzinger (8 April 1988) about progressivism and traditionalism in the church.[22] Recalling Jesus' promise to send the apostles the Spirit of truth, who would remain with them forever, the pope noted that the church has always been guided by faith in that promise, by the certainty that through the assistance of the Holy Spirit she will remain forever in the divine truth, preserving the apostolic succession through the college of bishops united with their head, the successor of Peter. The pope added:

> The Church manifested this conviction of faith also at the last Council, which met to reconfirm and reinforce the teaching of the Church inherited from the Tradition already existing for almost twenty centuries, as a living reality which progresses vis-a-vis the problems and needs of every age and deepens our understanding of what is already contained in the faith transmitted once and for all (cf. Jude 3).

After criticizing progressives in the church who fail to take into account Tradition's role in helping us continue in the truth transmitted by Christ and the apostles, the pope criticized those who simply equate Tradition with what is ancient.

> But it is not what is "ancient" as such, or what is "new" per se, which corresponds to the correct idea of Tradition in the life of the Church. Rather, that idea means the Church's remaining faithful to the truth received from God throughout the changing circumstances of history.

The pope ended this letter by asking Cardinal Ratzinger to continue his efforts to ensure ecclesial unity with the Priestly Fraternity of St. Pius X and Archbishop Lefebvre.

The following month the cardinal and the archbishop signed a document as a basis for that reconciliation, but a few days later Lefebvre disavowed that agreement. On 2 June 1988, the archbishop wrote to the pope, explaining that the moment of collaboration had not yet arrived, that false ecumenism was leading the church to ruin, and that Lefebvre and his followers needed protection against the spirit of Vatican II and the spirit of Assisi [site of the October 1986 prayer day for world peace hosted by Pope John Paul II for Christian and non-Christian religious leaders]. "We believe it is preferable to await a more propitious time for Rome's return to the Tradition," said the archbishop.[23] Although the pope responded with a letter asking Lefebvre not to begin a schism by ordaining bishops without papal permission, and although Vatican congregations and numerous conferences of bishops asked the archbishop not to carry out these ordinations, on June 30 he ordained four bishops from the Priestly Fraternity of St. Pius X. Lefebvre, the four new bishops and a bishop who had assisted as co-consecrator were automatically excommunicated by that action; Cardinal Gantin, prefect of the Congregation of Bishops, warned Catholics "not to support the schism of Monsignor Lefebvre, otherwise they shall incur ipso facto the very grave penalty of excommunication."[24]

In all his public statements and negotiations with the Vatican, Lefebvre protested that he was being faithful to the church's Tradition; the pope countered that Lefebvre was not the sole judge of that Tradition. The sad case of Archbishop Lefebvre illustrates the danger of one person assuming he alone is the arbiter of Tradition.

Being Faithful to the God of Both Testaments

Without the help of the community of believers, past and present, it is unlikely that any disciple of Jesus can be faithful to the richness of God's self-revelation offered in the Hebrew scriptures and in the New Testament. That revelation contains many complexities (most easily resolved by disregarding part of the scriptures!) that, if pondered with the help of the community of believers, can enrich the lives of individual Christians and the larger community.

The Christian community uses the scriptures in its liturgies and encourages bible study and scripturally-based prayer. Both Catholics and Protestants use a three-year cycle of scripture readings for the Sunday liturgy. More and more homilies are oriented to breaking open the word of God, to helping Christians make the connections between God's self-revelation in the scriptures and their daily lives. The Christian community encourages scholarly study of the scriptures, popular books and magazines that share the fruits of such study, and bible study groups.

The community that honors both testaments raises up individuals whose lives challenge any attempt to oversimplify the scriptures; for example, attempts to justify racism by saying that the members of the race considered inferior are the cursed descendants of Cain or the sons of Noah's son Ham.

In Chapter 1, I cited the example of a woman who questioned the value of prayer since she had prayed for a family situation for several years and the person died without any reconciliation. She said that when she telephoned a Christian radio program, she was told that she expected too much of God and that she should believe more firmly. She did not consider this response very helpful and sought a better answer from another believer. At times, smaller groups of Christians can misunderstand or distort the meaning of the scriptures, but the larger group has a sense of faith that can recognize distortions on major issues (Was Jesus really God or simply a good man? What good is praying when the result is not what we requested?).

Retreats, days of recollection, books, and magazines can all lead believers to understand how the scriptures may help them deal with personal or family crises. Of course meetings or writings that attribute all the world's problems to some type of conspiracy (the Jews, modernist Christians, fundamentalists, certain Christian churches) will simply confirm Christians in their spiritual blindness and selective reading of the scriptures.

In the sacrament of reconciliation and in pastoral counselling, oversimplifications of the scriptures can be addressed and the individual can receive help in dealing with various images of God. Since we act on the basis of our perceptions, correct or mistaken, the community of believers performs a vital role when it calls attention to our oversimplifications of the scriptures and shows us how to overcome them.

No one image of God is "it." We cannot disregard the Hebrew scriptures and pay attention only to the New Testament (as Marcion did). We cannot play off images of God in order to make our lives more simple.

How could we respect a God who could be captured in a single image? Although most Christians use more masculine than feminine images of God, does that mean God is masculine? Hardly. God is beyond our categories, and yet we must use verbal images if we are to speak about God and express our faith. We need both courage and modesty in our "God-talk." If we lack courage, we cannot communicate our faith. If we lack modesty in the way we speak about God, we may repeat the mistake of Job's friends, who loved their comfortable images of God more than the God who said that only Job had spoken correctly about him (Jb 42:7).

The mystery of the Trinity speaks of God as three Persons (Father, Son, and Holy Spirit), and yet these three Persons possess the same divine nature. A failure to distinguish the Persons would undermine the New Testament, but a failure to acknowledge their unity would create a dangerous oversimplification. Thus our language about the Trinity reflects both courage (certain images can be used) and modesty (any image has its limitations). The church's language about the Trinity and the theology behind that language has been refined in several hundred years of prayer and reflection. Christians *believed* in the Trinity long before they were satisfied with their *language* about it.

People who have one dominant image of God— Father, Shepherd, Healer—may become uncomfortable when, with the help of the scriptures and with their reflection on daily life, they see that that image needs to be complemented by another. They may feel disloyal to their religious upbringing; they might complain that they lack the religious fervor they once had. In fact, their faith could be experiencing growing pains. Theoretically we may tend to favor growth, but in practice we often find it messy and yearn for simpler days and a simpler faith.

The community of believers helps us deal with possible guilt feelings about accepting new images of God. Not every guilt feeling stems from some objective failing on our part, and the lack of guilt feelings does not necessarily indicate a clear conscience. A Christian racist may not feel guilty, but that does not mean that he or she is being faithful to the scriptures. And the Christian community needs to point that out.

I realize that in these pages I have spoken of the community of believers in an ideal sense. We all know that at times the church fails to challenge oversimplifications or does so in a clumsy way. Yet in the larger church there is an unerring sense of faith, an ability to distinguish what is faithful to the scriptures from what is not.

The community that identifies the scriptures for us can interpret those scriptures, can approve non-biblical language to explain its faith, and yet must exercise a certain caution about giving a monopoly to one theological perspective. If the community cannot be trusted to interpret the scriptures correctly, why should it be trusted to tell us that those writings are the word of God?

The same community that identifies for us the word of God can help us overcome communal and personal obstacles that prevent us from allowing that word to have its intended effect in our lives. The final chapter of this book will explore communal and personal issues we face as we grow with life and how we relate such growth to our growing with the scriptures.

For Personal Reflection

1. If we say that the scriptures are the church's book, does that influence the way I read them? What about the difficult parts?
2. Some people welcome paradoxical sayings about God. Others dislike them. Which am I? What are the possible dangers flowing from each preference?
3. Either/or thinking in the wrong place can be un-Christian. The same for both/and thinking. Have I ever used either style in the wrong context?
4. Simple answers to difficult questions are attractive but tend to lack holding power. Job told his comforters as much. Have I ever had a similar experience? Or have I been one of Job's "cruel comforters"? If so, what caused me to change my way of speaking about God?
5. Have I ever yearned for simpler days and a simpler faith? How did I handle the situation? What responses have I made to friends or relatives with the same yearnings?
6. In what ways are my knowledge of and love for the scriptures growing?

For Group Discussion

1. If our language about God is always partial and open to misunderstanding, why try to speak about God at all?
2. Why has Marcion's theory about a gracious New Testament God replacing a stern, legalistic Old Testament God been accepted in practice by many Christians—even if they have never heard of Marcion? How has that influenced our ways of talking about God?
3. We believe that God inspired four gospels instead of one. Does that tell me anything about God? about myself and others?
4. According to Frederick Sontag, "It is a perfectly healthy and natural phenomenon for some one concept of God to 'die,' and it tells us a great deal about our relationship to God." If someone is afraid to let any concept of God die, could he or she unintentionally be fostering atheism?
5. A truly Roman Catholic notion of Tradition sees it always in relation to the scriptures and to the church's teaching authority. What is the advantage of that approach over the simple identification of Tradition with the words and practices to which we have become very attached?
6. Why do we need both courage and modesty in the way we talk about God? What happens if either of those two virtues overwhelms the other?

Further Resources

Anthony E. Gilles, *Fundamentalism: What Every Catholic Needs to Know* (Cincinnati, OH: St. Anthony Messenger Press, 1985).

Eugene Maly, *The Word Alive* (Staten Island, NY: Alba House, 1982). Reflections on the Sunday and holy day scripture readings (all cycles).

Carlo Martini, *Journeying With the Lord: Everyday Meditations* (Staten Island, NY: Alba House, 1987).

Carlo Martini, *Through Moses to Jesus: The Way of the Paschal Mystery* (Notre Dame, IN: Ave Maria Press, 1988).

Carroll Stuhlmueller, C.P., *Biblical Meditations* (Mahwah, NJ: Paulist Press, 1984). This six-volume set summarizes the weekday and Sunday readings (all cycles) and gives a reflection for each day.

Francis A. Sullivan, S.J., *Magisterium: Teaching Authority in the Catholic Church* (Mahwah, NJ: Paulist Press, 1983).

SEVEN

Growing With Life

In *It Only Hurts When I Grow*, Father Kevin Kenny tells the stories of twenty young women and men who came to Covenant House to escape a life of teenage prostitution, chemical dependence, and the likelihood of a violent and premature death. Working as a chaplain there for six years, he saw thousands of young people on the edge of long-term decisions about their future. Some worked with the Covenant House program, but most returned to the streets. In any case personal growth was always exciting and often very painful; people tend to back away from it for fear it will hurt too much.

Especially in Florida, Arizona, and California, more and more people are deciding that growth and development are threatening to destroy the very qualities that attracted them to those communities, such as open spaces, clean air, and unpolluted water. Cities are beginning to take a much harder look at the tradeoffs involved with any growth.

In this chapter I will propose four group issues I consider very important for Christian faith today, issues intimately related to our images of God, self, and others. Readers may have resolved some of these issues for themselves long ago, but they remain "unfinished business" for many. This chapter will address very public issues, knowing full well that each reader may have significant private "unfinished business" about images of

God, self, and others. We cannot wait to resolve all the private issues before addressing the more public ones; indeed, the latter effort often helps to move the private ones toward an adequate solution. In this context *growing with life* means a willingness to deal with issues we once refused to face or considered irresoluble.

Is the Gospel a Western Monopoly?

Karl Rahner once observed that Vatican II marked the emergence of Catholicism as a world religion.[1] He said that the church's first phase (its birth from within Judaism) was quickly replaced by a Gentile-Roman-European orientation, which remained the standard for church thought and practice even when missionaries went to the Americas, to Africa, Asia, and Oceania. Many Protestant denominations have reflected the same Western perspective in preaching the good news.

That perspective is not evil in itself, but it is limited. To identify Christianity completely with a single culture means shackling the good news and making God that culture's greatest booster. Speaking of one country or another as a Christian country or a Catholic nation can lead to domesticating the gospel just as surely as the most hypocritical of the Pharisees denounced by Jesus had thoroughly domesticated the Mosaic Law to suit their own purposes. Those Pharisees had no "unfinished business" regarding faith and conversion, no room to grow except in observing the smaller parts of the Law more scrupulously while ignoring its more fundamental demands. Thus Jesus complained that the Pharisees paid tithes on the tiniest plants (dill, mint, and cumin) but ignored the weightier matters of the Law, such as justice and mercy.

The gospel is Western in the sense that it is addressed to Western peoples, and when they accept baptism and live out that commitment, they will do so largely within Western patterns of thought and worship. But the gospel is also Eastern, Northern, and Southern in those very same senses.

Perhaps nowhere are cultural differences more obvious than in liturgy, in the ways we celebrate God's saving love for us. Songs, vestments, liturgical postures and gestures, ways of speaking to and about God—all these reflect our cultural roots, the standards by which we judge things normal or not. While some Christians may regard variety in liturgical expression as a natural consequence of Jesus' incarnation, others secretly hope that believers from different cultures will eventually "give up their oddball behavior" and do things "the right way." On paper we may be all in favor of inculturation of the gospel, but in reality we may not be quite so open.

After twenty centuries, why is less than 18 percent of the world's population Christian? Why is less than 2.5 percent of Asia, which contains almost 60 percent of the world's population, Christian?[2] Why in many countries is becoming a Christian seen as part of the process of becoming Westernized, of losing one's native culture?

After the sixteenth century many European rulers saw religion as a way of reinforcing their control over native peoples. The implicit standard for the genuineness of their conversion was too often their ability to be "Western."

In the Introduction I mentioned Roland Joffee's movie "The Mission." That movie was based on the historical fact that in some parts of eighteenth-century South America the Jesuits were hated by Catholic rulers and colonists, who saw the Jesuit reductions (missions cut off from regular contact with European Christians) as subversive and a threat to good order. The campaign against the Jesuits became so intense that in 1773 the pope disbanded the Society of Jesus; a hundred years later the Jesuits had long been restored by another pope, yet those same colonial powers had lost control of many territories they had once ruled in the name of God and king. "The Mission" ends with the triumph of the colonial powers, the destruction of the reductions, and several Indian children picking up the musical and liturgical artifacts of a Christianity once friendly to their culture but no more. They return to the forest and to their pre-Christian ways.

In 1975 Pope Paul VI wrote *Evangelii Nuntiandi*, an apostolic letter about evangelization. The previous year the General Assembly of the Synod of Bishops had discussed that subject for a month and had given the pope various recommendations. *Evangelii Nuntiandi* squarely addresses the issue of inculturating the gospel:

> The Gospel and evangelization are not specially related to any culture but they are not necessarily incompatible with them. On the contrary, they can penetrate any culture while being subservient to none.[3]

Later in the same document he said that Jesus intended for his church to be "a universal Church knowing no bounds or limits except those, alas, which are to be found in the minds and hearts of sinful men."[4] The particular churches are advised to transpose the gospel message "into an idiom which will be understood by the people they serve."[5] Such transposing calls for prudence because evangelizers must take into account the people they are addressing (their language, their signs and symbols, their questions) without failing to present the entire gospel with all its challenges for every culture. Particular churches need to appreciate the universal dimension of the gospel and to make their proper, and therefore limited, contribution to that universality. An individual church that fails to appreciate the gospel's universality tends to become isolated and prone to factions since a divisive spirit tends to multiply itself.[6]

The 1985 General Assembly of the Synod of Bishops said that the church accepts whatever is positive in all cultures and affirmed that inculturation is not "a mere external adaptation."[7]

In 1987 the National Conference of Catholic Bishops (U.S.A.) issued "To the Ends of the Earth," a pastoral statement on world mission. After praising missionaries who have left their homeland to preach the gospel and to nurture local churches, the bishops noted:

> At times in the past missionaries brought not only the strengths but also some of the weaknesses of Western civilization. It often happened that they labored in lands where their own country had political and economic interests. In areas where their home country was the colonial power, those to whom they were sent sometimes found it difficult to distinguish the church's missionary effort from the colonizing effort, which proved critical when the colonial empires were dismantled after World War II.[8]

Today missionaries must face the challenge "of clearly distinguishing their Christian mission from colonial and neocolonial practices."[9] "The ground in which we are called to plant the Gospel is holy ground," the bishops said, "for before our arrival God has already visited the people he knows and loves."[10] The church must be a leaven for all cultures, at home in every culture.

> True inculturation occurs when the Gospel penetrates the heart of cultural experience and shows how Christ gives new meaning to authentic human values. However, the church must never allow herself to be absorbed by any culture, since

not all cultural expressions are in conformity
with the Gospel.[11]

That final caution applies both to the native culture of
the missionary and to the native culture of those being
evangelized.

Our images of God, self, and others are related to
the way we think and speak about the church, which
is called to announce the good news of Jesus Christ.
On the level of official documents the Roman Catholic
Church's leadership has already said most of the right
things about inculturation, but that does not automatically change the hearts and minds of its members. Conversion on this issue is just beginning for many, many
people. Inculturation of the gospel will be a very live
issue for the foreseeable future, with enormous implications for our images of God, ourselves, and others.

Is God Male?

Although the answer to this question is obviously
no, there is a strong tendency to speak of God in male
terms. In the patriarchal society in which biblical revelation began, it was easy to assume that an all-powerful
God would resemble the people who made the laws and
major decisions in that culture: men. Here we may have
the shadow side of inculturation, in which God's self-
revelation can be stunted by the culture to which it is
addressed. That culture may be willing to hear only what
reinforces its present beliefs. Even so, the creation stories
in the Book of Genesis present Adam and Eve as equal
in dignity—at a time when most cultures did not believe
that men and women had a common origin or dignity,
much less a common destiny of life with God.

In *Women's Reality*, Anne Wilson Schaef describes
an exercise she has often used in workshops given to
church, business, and government groups. Using a

chalkboard she heads one column "God" and the other "Humankind"; she then asks participants to describe God, and humankind in relation to God. Believers, agnostics, and atheists tend to produce the very same lists, she reports. Then she asks workshop participants to suggest adjectives that describe males, and females in relation to males. When the four lists are put side by side, they usually read:

God	Humankind	Male	Female
male	childlike	intelligent	emotional
omnipotent	sinful	powerful	weak
omniscient	weak	brave	fearful
omnipresent	stupid or	good	sinful
immortal	dumb	strong	like children
eternal	mortal		

She says that the obvious conclusion from such lists is that "male is to female as God is to humankind." She describes such thinking as the white male system in which men strive for divinity and die in the process, but women have no chance to strive for divinity. Thus their way of relating to men reflects this presumed inequality.[12]

We cannot communicate except through signs, symbols, and words. Thus, unless we are ready to quit talking about God, we must use our limited supply of signs, symbols, words—and the images that underlie them. But if we forget that our images are always incomplete, that they always leave something important unsaid, we are flirting with disaster, with the possibility of loving our images and our language about God more than we love God. Job's friends show us where such stubbornness can lead.

In *Women and the Word*, scripture scholar Sandra Schneiders says that although our metaphors about God have the advantage of concretely appealing to our minds and affections, of shaping our images of God, they are also dangerous because they can easily be taken literally.

> While we are immediately aware that the personal God is not really a rock or a mother eagle, it is easy enough to imagine that God is really a king or a father. A literalized metaphor paralyzes the imagination. Instead of functioning as an ever-active incentive to affective reflection on the inexhaustible mystery of the godhead, it traps the mind in a limited and therefore untrue conception of God.[13]

To avoid this danger we have to admit the limits of our metaphors; for example, it is equally true to say that God is not our father as it is to say that God is our father.

An additional problem with religious metaphors is that they tend to work simultaneously in two directions.

> We create the metaphor to say something about God; but then God seems to be saying something about the vehicle of the metaphor. Thus, if God is a king, there is a tendency to see kings as divine. If God is male, then males are divine and masculinity becomes normative of humanity, the true image of God.[14]

After pointing out seven passages in the Hebrew scriptures in which female imagery is applied to God,[15] Schneiders says that those scriptures do not use male imagery to portray God as a patriarch in relation to the Hebrews. Next she points out that Jesus did not present God in exclusively masculine terms (being born again in the Holy Spirit and the woman searching for the lost coin); the male metaphors about God cannot be made literal or absolute.

At his Angelus address on 10 September 1978, Pope John Paul I spoke of presidents Carter and Sadat and

Prime Minister Begin meeting at Camp David, working and praying for peace. The pope cited Isaiah's question, "Can a mother forget her own child? But even if it should happen, God will never forget his people" (Is 49:15). The pope continued:

> Also we who are here have the same sentiments; we are the objects of undying love on the part of God. We know: he has always his eyes open to us, even when it seems to be dark. He is our father; even more he is our mother. He does not want to hurt us. He wants only to do good to us, to all of us. If children are ill, they have additional claims to be loved by their mother. And we too, if by chance we are sick with badness, on the wrong track, have yet another claim to be loved by the Lord.[16]

The scriptures obviously use more male imagery about God than female imagery, but the latter imagery is there and is perhaps all the more remarkable because it arose in a male-dominated society and is accepted by Christians as part of God's self-revelation.

Being Individuals and Part of a Community: Our Love/Hate Relationship

Our images of God can easily reflect our ambiguity about ourselves as individuals and as members of a faith community. In many ways the either/or option (individual *or* member of a community) is easier than the both/and option (individual *and* member of a community).

However, destroying the tension between these polarities is a dangerous, short-term victory. It leaves us defenseless should selfishness ever present itself as heroic or should respect for the group ever lead to a denial of what we believe in good conscience to be true and morally good.

Adults like to think of themselves as superior to teenagers, who are struggling to shape their personal identity, to explore for themselves the individual/group polarity. But in fact many adults have a love/hate relationship with that same polarity. Our advertising tends to emphasize the advantages of being one's own person—by joining the group of people who smoke the same cigarettes, use the same perfume or aftershave, or drive the same kind of car. We like both the sense of personal responsibility *and* the safety of knowing that many other people have made the same choice. Although we tend to fear being manipulated by or becoming an anonymous part of big government, big business, huge hospitals, or mega-universities, most people enjoy the advantages that come from working for a large business, going to a large school, or being insured by a well-known company.

If we choose one side of the individual/group polarity and deny the other side, our images of God will probably fall neatly into place. God might become the ultimate non-conformist, encouraging us to shout "I've got to be me" (in a very ruthless way) and to insist "That's your problem" whenever some difficult situation arises. Or else God could become the ultimate household deity, forever sanctioning "what everyone knows" and branding as blasphemous any challenge to the group's cozy descriptions of God. A community that ruthlessly punishes anyone who thinks and talks in new ways is, in fact, acknowledging the value of the individual—in a backhanded way. If the individual were not important, there would be no need to demand perfect agreement on all matters.

That is not to say that every image of God is equally valid. When some people speak about God sending suffering in order to test people, that suggests to me a ten-year-old sadist who takes a magnifying glass on a sunny day to see how ants on the sidewalk react to an intense concentration of light and heat. The scriptures are much more sophisticated in speaking about suffering as a test than most people realize. God is not a sadist who enjoys watching people suffer.

Unfinished business tends to generate more unfinished business. If we feel threatened by people with a strong sense of their own individuality or by communities with a strong sense of their reason for existence, our images of God will tend to reflect that fear, that love/hate relationship or our decision to solve the difficulty by denying one side of the polarity. Such a solution has radical implications for people who identify themselves as Christians.

Tensions Within the Church: Being Tempted to Use God as a Club

One way of dealing with tensions in the church is to assume that everyone who does not agree with me has faulty images of God, images which, if corrected, would lead them immediately to accept my viewpoint. I can use my images of God to question other people's sincerity, pressuring them to see things my way and act accordingly—no matter which side of the individual/group polarity I might favor.

For example, if I consistently resolve the individual/group polarity in my own favor, I will probably become a perpetual critic of what the church does or does not do—all the while holding myself above the messiness that belonging to a group always involves. On the other hand, if I consistently resolve that same polarity in favor of the church as I understand it at this moment, I risk becoming a Pharisee in the worst sense of the term: someone who identifies his or her own agenda completely with God's agenda. Some examples of both extremes may be useful here.

Haven't all of us experienced other people (and maybe ourselves) quite eager to castigate the church for failings, such as bad popes, the Inquisition, financial mismanagement, or denying religious freedom to other religious groups—without admitting that the church (we) have contributed to the more modern failings? Why don't "they" do something about these things? Why don't the bishops bring about the changes I would most like to see effected? Why aren't the people in the pews more responsive to the issues I consider important? Why should I get involved with a church whose leaders and members are so imperfect? Why should I spend time on someone else's agenda when I know that mine is all-embracing?

On the other hand, haven't we all known people (perhaps ourselves) who immediately invoke the group's authority the minute one of their pet ideas is questioned? Haven't we ever seen the valid concern for orthodoxy used in an un-Christian way? Haven't we ever seen the modern equivalent of the priest Amaziah telling Amos to prophesy somewhere else because Bethel was a royal sanctuary—where one should say only what pleases the king and his advisors?

Within the Roman Catholic Church since Vatican II, some tensions have arisen over the meaning and interpretation of that council—tensions related to our images of God, the church, and of ourselves.

In 1985 the General Assembly of the Synod of Bishops drew up a report on twenty years of implementing Vatican II, noting that the church has experienced many benefits from that council. The bishops also observed that many internal difficulties since 1965 have been caused by "the partial and selective reading of the

Council, and the superficial interpretation of its teachings in one or the other sense."[17] The synod members cautioned against separating the pastoral character from the doctrinal force of the Vatican II documents and against opposing the spirit and the letter of the council. Later the synod said that the church possessed both unity and pluriformity understood in the correct sense.[18] How can Catholics recognize such unity and pluriformity unless their images of God are both orthodox and open to growth?

In 1987 another General Assembly of the Synod of Bishops addressed "The Vocation and Mission of the Laity in the Church and in the World Twenty Years After the Second Vatican Council." In their "Message to the People of God," the synod members said that lay women and men, with the help of their bishops' discernment, "learn to recognize the spiritual gifts with which the Lord has enriched us for the good of the community of faith and the global society."[19] From such gifts and charisms "flow associations and movements which effectively work together for the building up of the Church." The Holy Spirit raises up new movements "which fill the universal Church with joy and hope. Working in harmony in the local Church with their Pastors to build the Church in love and unity will always be a valid criterion of their authenticity."

What "associations and movements" are meant here? Any that identify themselves with the Roman Catholic Church, for example, Opus Dei, Communion and Liberation, charismatic renewal groups, new religious communities, or associations of Catholics. Why did the 1987 synod stress the need to work in harmony with local bishops as a criterion of the group's authenticity? It seems to me that the synod members wanted to ensure that such associations and movements would, from the beginning, have to deal with a larger church and larger images of God than if those groups developed apart from the local bishops. Otherwise a warped picture of one's own movement and its relation to the rest of the church could end in self-righteousness and division.

I am convinced that Francis of Assisi aided the church in the thirteenth century precisely because he insisted on working with the local bishops and with the popes—none of whom was perfect. But then neither was Francis, and he knew it. Self-righteousness was not his style, and those prone to it either changed or eventually parted company with Francis.

In recent years the United States Catholic Bishops have written two pastoral letters, "The Challenge of Peace: God's Promise and Our Response" and "Economic Justice for All: Catholic Social Teaching and the U.S. Economy." These letters have led some Catholics to object that the bishops have strayed from their proper responsibilities and have engaged in partisan proposals about politically sensitive topics. The bishops have answered that criticism by pointing out the non-negotiable demands of the gospel and the legitimate differences Christians may have about how best to make those gospel values a reality. Is it possible that the bishops and these critics are proceeding from different images of God, themselves, and the church—and thus are bound to arrive at very different conclusions? Some of those same critics were no happier with Pope John Paul II's encyclical *Sollicitudo Rei Socialis* (1988), saying that his harsh words about capitalism arise from a misunderstanding of that socio-economic system. In fact, in two previous encyclicals the pope has spoken knowledgeably about the failures of capitalism and communism to respect the total dignity of the person.[20]

Unfinished Personal Business

In this chapter I have addressed four issues that remain unfinished business for many Christians. Many other more personal issues may lie dormant on our agenda, stunting our images of God, sapping our energy for personal growth and conversion. One person overwhelmed by fear of an unforgiven sin, another person still feeling the sting of praying for something very important and not getting it, an adult child of an alcoholic parent, an elderly man or woman absorbed by fear of ill health—all these people have major, unfinished personal business, which may hinder them from growing in their interlocking images of God, self, and others. I cannot propose here a single method or procedure for bringing a healthy closure to those situations and for continuing to grow as persons, as believers in the God of the scriptures, as responsible citizens, and as loving neighbors. Each person who wants to resolve such unfinished personal business must seek out the resources he or she considers most likely to be helpful.

No matter how hard we may try to resolve personal issues, which may have been on the back burner of life for months or years, we should not think that having such unfinished business means we have necessarily neglected the scriptures or the demands of Christian discipleship today. The wonderful variety of images of God in the Hebrew and Christian scriptures arises partly from the dissatisfaction of some biblical authors with the conventional images of God presented to them. Those responsible for the four theological traditions in the Pentateuch were growing with their life experiences; divine inspiration works with the human maturing process rather than replacing it. The prophets often had very painful life experiences (Hosea's unfaithful wife, Ezekiel's exile, Jeremiah's loneliness in his prophetic

mission), but their growth in those circumstances was related to the divinely-inspired message they have left us.
Whoever wrote the Book of Job probably knew innocent
human suffering at very close range; the writer's personal crisis did not stifle God's self-revelation. Matthew,
Mark, Luke, and John, and the faith communities they
addressed, knew painful challenges to faith and worked
through them.

The idea of God serenely guiding the hand of the
inspired writers may be replaced by God helping the inspired writer to face his or her challenges to faith and to
record a message needed for future believers. God's self-
revelation, a healthy image of oneself, a truthful image of
others—these do not happen after the crises of daily life
are handled but rather as we handle them, discovering
strengths and weaknesses previously unforeseen.

Discipleship: Growing Until We
See God Face to Face

In Chapter 1, I said that the person whose image of
God is contradicted by a new and painful experience has
the same options, in a sense, as the person who outgrows
a pair of shoes: 1) continue to wear the same shoes and
complain that they do not fit (why is God punishing
me?); 2) quit wearing shoes (become an atheist or an
agnostic); or 3) find shoes that fit (grow in my images
of God and their impact on my image of myself and
others).

I find this analogy useful; however, unlike feet,
one's images of God need not stop growing. When
St. Paul told the Christians in Philippi to imitate Christ's
self-emptying, wasn't the apostle describing a discipleship where growth is a standard feature rather than an
option? If we continue to follow the example of Jesus,
one day we shall see God face to face; only then will our
images of God, self, and others be complete. If we should

refuse a healthy, growing discipleship, we could be lost eternally, forever misunderstanding God, ourselves, and others, accumulating a lifetime of illusions and grudges.

After seven years of constructing the Temple in Jerusalem, King Solomon finished this magnificent symbol of God's presence and abiding love for the Hebrew people. At the dedication of the Temple, Solomon prayed:

> Will God really live with people on earth? Why, the heavens and the heavens of the heavens cannot contain you! How much less this temple built by me! Even so, listen favorably to the prayer and entreaty of your servant, Yahweh my God; listen to the cry and to the prayer which your servant makes to you. Day and night, may your eyes watch over this temple, over this place in which you have promised to put your name. Listen to the prayer which your servant offers in this place (2 Chr 6:18–20).

Just as Solomon's Temple did not confine God, so Solomon's words did not confine God either. Our language is useful but never absolutely faithful to God's ways. Years later Solomon built temples for other gods and prayed to them. Was the prayer quoted above worthwhile? Certainly. Was it enough for a lifetime of being faithful to the Lord's ways? No.

Yesterday's prayer may make today's easier, but it cannot make today's prayer unnecessary. A sense of "having it made" regarding one's images of God, self, and others can only spell disaster. The Pharisee praying at the front of the Temple "had it made." The tax collector praying in the back was still growing.

While I offer no simple formula for growing in our images of God, I would suggest that we need to
1. keep praying,
2. keep reading the scriptures and meditating on them,

3. keep exploring the meaning of our faith, and
4. keep allowing faith to overflow with the corporal and
   spiritual works of mercy.

Perseverance is central to growing in our images of God.
The evangelist Luke does not tell us that the Virgin Mary
understood immediately what God asked of her or that
Mary never had a difficult moment in her discipleship.
What Luke does tell us is that Mary "treasured all these
things and pondered them in her heart" (Lk 2:19). In
the treasuring and the pondering she became a disciple,
growing in her images of God, herself, and others—and
so will we.

For Personal Reflection

1. Is my God very Western? Do I feel threatened by Christians
   whose God is not so Western?
2. Have I ever met a Christian who spoke about and prayed
   to God in a way which I found foreign? How did I react?
3. How do I feel when someone speaks of God as mother?
4. Any one image of God leaves many important things unsaid. Am I willing to accept several images in order to be
   more truthful about God, myself, and others? What changes
   may I have to make in order to do that? Are there some
   images of God I should not accept?
5. To which side of the individual/group polarity am I usually
   attracted? Has that preference ever caused me to ignore
   some valid concern on the other side of this polarity?
6. Do I have some unfinished personal business hampering
   my relationship with God? with my own self-esteem? my
   relationships with others? In what ways am I growing with
   life? not growing with life?

For Group Discussion

1. Does the custom of referring to countries as "a Christian
   country" or "a Catholic country" subtly suggest that the
   people there have already fully converted to the gospel?

2. Are there ways in which the good news of Jesus challenges common assumption of our culture? If so, in what ways?
3. Go back and reread Anne Wilson Schaef's lists on page 169. Would your group produce a similar list? What does that mean about your images of God, yourself, and others?
4. Is God equally mother and father? Why has the mother image been difficult for some people to accept? Why have other people found the father image difficult to accept?
5. Were the United States bishops fulfilling or straying from their responsibilities when they wrote their 1983 pastoral letter about war and peace, and their 1986 pastoral letter about Catholic social teaching and the United States economy? Why or why not?
6. Have we sometimes acted as if our words and actions could contain God, that is, totally represent God and the divine intention for the world?

Further Resources

Jean Acheson, *Portraits of Healing, Prayers of Wholeness* (Notre Dame, IN: Ave Maria Press, 1989).

Carlo Carretto, *Journey Without End* (Notre Dame, IN: Ave Maria Press, 1989).

Elizabeth Dreyer, *Passionate Women: Two Medieval Mystics* (Mahwah, NJ: Paulist Press, 1989).

Barbara Fiand, S.N.D. de N., *Embracing the Feminine in a Masculine Culture: A First Step Toward Wholeness*, audiocassette (Cincinnati, OH: St. Anthony Messenger Press, 1988).

Thomas Green, S.J., *Come Down Zacchaeus: Spirituality and the Laity* (Notre Dame, IN: Ave Maria Press, 1988).

Gerard Hughes, *God of Surprises* (Mahwah, NJ: Paulist Press, 1985).

Kevin Kenny, with Dorianne Perrucci, *It Only Hurts When I Grow* (Mahwah, NJ: Paulist Press, 1988).

Martha Ann Kirk, *God of Our Mothers: Seven Biblical Women Tell Their Stories*, audiocassette (Cincinnati, OH: St. Anthony Messenger Press, 1985).

Matthew Linn, S.J., Sheila Fabricant, and Dennis Linn, S.J., *Healing the Eight Stages of Life* (Mahwah, NJ: Paulist Press, 1987).

Johannes Metz, *Poverty of Spirit* (Mahwah, NJ: Paulist Press, 1968).

Carolyn Osiek, *Beyond Anger: On Being a Feminist in the Church* (Mahwah, NJ: Paulist Press, 1986).

Martin Pable, OFM Cap., *A Man and His God: Contemporary Male Spirituality* (Notre Dame, IN: Ave Maria Press, 1988).

Beth Ann Rufo, and Raymond Rufo, *Called and Gifted: Lay Spirituality in Ordinary Life* (South Orange, NJ: Pillar Books, 1988).

Richard Sweeney, *Spirituality and the Seasons of Adulthood*, audiocassette (Cincinnati, OH: St. Anthony Messenger Press, 1986).

Woman Sharing About God, Prayer, Jesus, Self, Service, audiocassette (Cincinnati, OH: St. Anthony Messenger Press, 1988).

Appendix

Applying human characteristics to God may strike some people as dangerous or bordering on idolatry. But both the Hebrew Scriptures and the New Testament frequently accept that risk in the hope of better communicating what kind of a God has created the world, makes covenants, and desires that we all share in divine life.

The following chart illustrates several common physical characteristics which the scriptures apply to God.

	Total number of times this word is used	Total usage in relation to God	Used in Hebrew Scriptures	Used in the New Testament
BREATH	69	15	15	0
EYE	83	3	3	0
EYES	471	62	52	10
EARS	101	12	10	2
FEET	239	10	10	0
HAND	846	224	201	23
HANDS	471	39	36	3
MOUTH	266	29	28	1
NOSTRILS	12	1	1	0
VOICE	301	115	92	23
TOTAL		510	448	62

Since the New Testament details the revelation of Jesus Christ as the Son of God, we would expect fewer anthropomorphisms there.

Writing in the Jerome Biblical Commentary (article 77:21), John L. McKenzie notes that applying human characteristics to nonhuman beings

> is common in both religious and profane literatures of all cultures. What makes anthropomorphisms worthy of special attention in the Old Testament is the difficulty of reconciling it with the prohibition of images and the explicit denials that Yahweh is like any created being. The fear of a plastic image of Yahweh is in marked contrast

with the lack of restraint in employing verbal images. Yahweh has a countenance, eyes, ears, mouth, nostrils, hands, feet. He speaks, hears, smells, laughs, hisses, whistles, strikes, writes, walks. He feels delight, joy, anger, hatred, love, disgust, regret, compassion. The Old Testament never speaks of Yahweh without attributing human traits to him.

Although the scriptures often apply human characteristics to God, the biblical writers realized that these figures of speech have their limitations. In the Jerome Biblical Commentary article quoted above, McKenzie cites three passages which reveal that caution: Yahweh is not changeable or infirm of purpose like man (Nm 23:19), that he is elohim and not man (Hos 11:9), and that Yahweh is spirit and not flesh (Is 31:3).

Although some people may be tempted to dismiss the application of human characteristics to God as "mere poetry," such an attitude can easily suggest that only mathematical equations and things which can be weighed and measured are "real." Such an approach to life enables the mathematician, the astronomer, and the physicist to do their jobs very carefully, but those same people have a life beyond the strictly professional. Can anyone afford to dismiss as "mere poetry" whatever does not meet such an impoverished definition of reality?

If God is interested in self-revelation, then God must, to some extent, submit to human metaphors and imagery. Otherwise, we can have only a very aloof God who is interested in the cosmos but not in the lives of individuals and nations.

The word counts used in the chart above are based on: Nelson's Complete Concordance of the New American Bible, edited by Stephen Hartdegen, OFM (Nashville, TN: Thomas Nelson Inc., Publishers, 1977).

Endnotes

Chapter 1—Is Your God Too Small?

[1] Pat McCloskey, O.F.M., *When You Are Angry With God* (Mahwah, NJ: Paulist Press, 1987).

[2] Harold S. Kushner, *When Bad Things Happen to Good People* (New York: Avon Books, 1983), 138.

[3] Gustavo Gutierrez has written an excellent book on the various theologies at stake in the Book of Job. See *On Job: God-Talk and the Suffering of the Innocent* (Maryknoll, NY: Orbis Books, 1987).

[4] For another perspective on scripture's use of suffering as a test, see McCloskey, 37–40. See also "suffering" in the index of major footnotes in *The New Jerusalem Bible* (New York: Doubleday and Company, 1985) and in the index of *The Jerome Biblical Commentary* (Englewood Cliffs: Prentice-Hall, 1968).

[5] Bishops' Commission for Ecumenical and Interreligious Affairs, *Criteria for the Evaluation of Dramatizations of the Passion* (Washington, DC: United States Catholic Conference, 1988). This document points out (p.8) that Jesus should not be portrayed as opposed to or by the Pharisees as a group. Jesus shared important Pharisaic doctrines that set them apart from other Jewish groups of the time, such as the Sadducees. *The New Jerusalem Bible* has five major footnotes explaining the Pharisee movement. See also, "A History of Israel," article 75, nos. 120–22 in *The Jerome Biblical Commentary*.

[6] Studs Terkel, *American Dreams: Lost and Found* (New York: Pantheon Books, 1980), 146.

[7] Sister Suzanne's story appeared in the *Catholic Telegraph* (Cincinnati, Ohio) on 9 January 1987. Rafe Middeke wrote the original story for *The Messenger*, newspaper of the diocese of Belleville, Illinois.

Chapter 2—Images of God in the Hebrew Scriptures

[1] The Yahwist account regarding the change of names from Jacob to Israel appears in Gn 32:25–31, the Elohist account in Gn 35:9–15. Other doublets concern the genealogies of Cain, the covenant with Abraham, the dismissal of Hagar and the call of Moses. *The New Jerusalem Bible*, "Introduction to the Pentateuch," 8.

[2] Ibid. 5–16.

[3] *The New Jerusalem Bible,* 41, footnote 22. See also articles 1, 66, 70, 71 in *The Jerome Biblical Commentary.*

[4] Bruce Vawter, C.M., *A Path Through Genesis* (New York: Sheed and Ward, 1956), 169.

[5] *The New Jerusalem Bible,* 274.

[6] *The New Jerusalem Bible,* 1162.

[7] God's faithful love for Israel is a major theme in the Hebrew scriptures, e.g., in Is 54:8, Jer 31:31ff and Ez 36:25ff. See *The New Jerusalem Bible,* 1274. The theme is repeated in the New Testament. See *The New Jerusalem Bible,* 1873.

[8] Israel is described as a vine in Jer 2:21, Ez 15:1, and Hos 10:1; the same imagery is applied to the royal house of Judah in Ez 19:10. In the parable of the wicked tenants (Mt 26:33–44, Mk 12:1–11 and Lk 20:9–18), Israel is a vineyard neglected by its original tenants and given to new ones. In Jn 15:1–17, Jesus calls himself the true vine from which the disciples receive life.

[9] The four songs of the Servant of Yahweh are found in Is 42:1–4; 49:1–7; 50:4–11 and 52:13—53:12.

[10] *The New Jerusalem Bible,* 1189.

[11] Ibid. 965.

[12] Cf. Jer 17:14–18, Is 14:12–15, 47:1–15, and Ps 10, 22, 35, 37.

Chapter 3—Images of God in the New Testament

[1] This choice obviously does not do justice to the rich images of God found in other New Testament writings; for example, John's gospel stresses Jesus as the incarnate Word of the Father (1:1–18), the bread of life (6:30–37), the light of the world (8:12) to name only a few such images.

[2] *The New Jerusalem Bible,* 1992.

[3] The *anawim* were men and women ready to submit to the will of God, even if it meant becoming poor and humble for the sake of others. The notion of poverty as a curse from God begins to change in the prophets, especially in Psalm 34 and in Zephaniah. Cf. *The New Jerusalem Bible,* 1569, and *The Jerome Biblical Commentary,* article 59, section 10. The concept of the *anawim* is one of the most obvious links between the Hebrew scriptures and the New Testament.

[4] This verse is an allusion to Ezekiel 34, where God proclaims that he will shepherd his own people because Israel's kings have, as a group, failed as shepherds. The image of Jesus as the good shepherd is strongly developed in the gospel of John, chapter 10.

Chapter 4—Images of God, Ourselves, and Others: What Relation?

[1] Flannery O'Connor, "Revelation" in *Complete Stories of Flannery O'Connor* (New York: Farrar, Straus and Giroux, 1971), 490. The other quotations from that story appear on pages 488–509.

[2] Flannery O'Connor, *The Habit of Being*, ed. Sally Fitzgerald (New York: Farrar, Straus and Giroux, 1979), 93.

[3] Ibid. 131.

[4] *The Confessions of St. Augustine*, trans. John K. Ryan (New York: Doubleday and Company, 1960). A translation by Frank Sheed was reissued by Sheed and Ward in 1988.

[5] Regis Armstrong, O.F.M. Cap., and Ignatius Brady, O.F.M., *Francis and Clare: The Complete Works* (Mahwah, NJ: Paulist Press, 1982), 154.

[6] Marion Habig, O.F.M., ed., *St. Francis of Assisi: Writings and Early Biographies* (Chicago: Franciscan Herald Press, 1973), 318 (2 Celano 103).

[7] *Challenge to the Church: A Theological Comment on the Political Crisis in South Africa* (Grand Rapids, MI: Wm B. Eerdmans Publishing Co., 1985).

[8] Ibid. chap. 1.

[9] Ibid. 2.2.4.

[10] Ibid.

[11] Ibid.

[12] *Evangelical Witness in South Africa* (Grand Rapids, MI: Wm. B. Eerdmans Publishing Co., 1986), preface.

[13] Ibid.

[14] Ibid.

[15] Ibid.

[16] Ibid.

[17] Ibid. See also "The Road to Damascus: Kairos and Conversion" (Washington, D.C.: Center for Concern, 1989). Christians from seven Third World countries critique right-wing Christianity.

[18] "Confrontation," *Les Miserables* (music by Claude-Michel Schonberg and lyrics by Herbert Kretzmer, copyright David Greffen Company, 1987).

[19] Ibid. "Stars."

Chapter 5—Prayer and Our Images of God

[1] John Sanford, *The Man Who Wrestled With God: Light from the Old Testament on the Psychology of Individuation* (Mahwah, NJ: Paulist Press, 1981), 38.

2 McCloskey, 74–89.

3 Habig, 1501–2.

4 Habig, (2 Celano 158), 489.

5 See Kieran Kavanaugh's introduction to *The Interior Castle* (Mahwah, NJ: Paulist Press, 1979). See also Teresa's *Way of Perfection*, trans. Alice Alexander (Westminster, MD: Newman Bookshop, 1946).

6 Alexander, 168.

7 Kavanaugh, xvii.

8 See Boniface Hanley, O.F.M., *Ten Christians* (Notre Dame, IN: Ave Maria Press, 1979), 67–92, for a short life of Frederick Ozanam.

9 See Dorothy Day, *The Long Loneliness* (New York: Harper and Row, 1952); William Miller, *Dorothy Day: A Biography* (New York: Harper and Row, 1982), and Jim Forest, *Love Is the Measure* (Mahwah, NJ: Paulist Press, 1986).

10 Forest, 205.

11 For background on Archbishop Desmond Tutu, see *Current Biography Yearbook 1985*, 418–21; *International Who's Who*, 1505.

12 *London Observer* (8 May 1983), 7. Quoted in *Current Biography Yearbook 1985* (New York: Wilson, 1985), 418.

13 *Current Biography*, 419.

14 Desmond Tutu, *Hope and Suffering* (Grand Rapids, MI: Wm. B. Eerdmans Publishing Co., 1984), 155.

15 *Current Biography*, 421.

16 Tutu, 136.

17 For background on Simone Weil, see Dorothy Tuck Mc-Farland, *Simone Weil* (New York: Crossroad/Continuum Publishing Group, 1983); G. Thibon and J. M. Perrin, *Simone Weil as We Knew Her* (London: Routledge and Kegan Paul, 1953); Simone Petrement, *Simone Weil: A Life* (New York: Pantheon Books, 1976); Joseph Goetz, *Mirrors of God* (Cincinnati, OH: St. Anthony Messenger Press, 1984); Simone Weil, *Waiting for God* (New York: Harper and Row, 1973); and Simone Weil, *Gateway to God* (Glasgow: William Collins Sons & Co. Ltd, 1974).

18 Weil, *Waiting for God*, 52–53.

19 Ibid. 74.

20 Kenneth Allott, *The Poems of Matthew Arnold* (New York: Barnes and Noble, Inc., 1965), 285–94.

21 Kushner, 138.

Chapter 6—Growing With the Scriptures

[1] Maria Leach, *Noodles, Nitwits and Numskulls* (New York: Dell, 1979), 54.

[2] Robert Murray, S.J., "Do We Still Need the Old Testament?" *Month* (June 1986), 199. This article provides a good summary of Marcion's teaching.

[3] Ibid.

[4] Ibid.

[5] Pope John Paul II, 15 October 1988 address to the New York bishops on an ad limina visit, *L'Osservatore Romano*, English edition (24 October 1988), 22.

[6] Murray, 200.

[7] See Richard McBrien, *Catholicism* (Minneapolis: Winston Press, 1980), 1174–75 on the both/and approach as characteristic of Catholicism. Earlier in that same book McBrien describes three approaches to the church based on how one thinks that it relates to human history (classicism, historicism, and historical consciousness). I think that the historical consciousness approach favored in recent years is much more inclined to the both/and style of thinking than the classicist approach, which tends toward the either/or style. See also Bernard Lonergan, S.J., *Method in Theology* (New York: Harper and Row, 1979) regarding the classicist approach to history and theology.

[8] For a longer treatment on Stoicism and its influence within Christianity, see McCloskey, 68–72; John L. McKenzie, "The World of the New Testament" in *The Power and the Wisdom: An Interpretation of the New Testament* (Milwaukee, WI: Bruce, 1965).

[9] Eugene Maly, "The Gift of the Spirit: Biblical Times and Today," audiocassette (Cincinnati, OH: St. Anthony Messenger, 1974). This tape is no longer in print, but it can be found in some tape libraries. Maly credited the inclusivist/correlative/exclusivist terminology to W.C. Smith's talk, "The Spirit and Power and Christian Secularity," at a University of Notre Dame symposium.

[10] Frederick Sontag, *The God of Evil: An Argument From the Existence of the Devil* (New York: Harper and Row, 1970), 31.

[11] Ibid. 53–54.

[12] *Declaration on the Relationship of the Church to Non-Christian Religions* (*Nostra Aetate*), section 4, in Walter Abbott, S.J., ed., *The Documents of Vatican II* (New York: America Press, 1966), 665–66.

[13] Bishops' Committee for Ecumenical and Interreligious Affairs, "Criteria for the Evaluation of Dramatizations of the Passion"

Pub. No. 211-X (Washington, DC: United States Catholic Conference, 1988), 3.

[14] Ibid. 7.

[15] Ibid. 8.

[16] Ibid. 9.

[17] Ibid. 11. The attempt to reduce the four accounts of Jesus' passion to a single text indicates an uneasiness with both/and thinking and a preference for either/or thinking.

[18] Raymond E. Brown, S.S., *The Churches the Apostles Left Behind* (Mahwah, NJ: Paulist Press, 1984).

[19] Raymond E. Brown, S.S., *Biblical Exegesis and Church Doctrine* (Mahwah, NJ: Paulist Press, 1985), 126. After a chapter on critical biblical exegesis and the development of doctrine, Brown devotes separate chapters to the liberal and the conservative misunderstandings of the interaction between biblical criticism and dogma.

[20] Lefebvre used this expression during his homily on 29 June 1976 when he ordained his first priests against the pope's wishes. See McCloskey, "Tradition: What Is It? Who Needs It?" *St. Anthony Messenger* (August 1977), 40–44.

[21] Pope Paul VI, *Origins* 6:26 (16 December 1976): 417–18.

[22] This letter appears in the *L'Osservatore Romano*, English edition (18 April 1988), 2. The three quotations from this letter all appear on page 1 of that edition. The complete text appears in *Origins* 17:46 (28 April 1988): 803–4.

[23] This letter is quoted in the 17 June 1988 Informatory Note issued by the Vatican Press Office and printed in the *L'Osservatore Romano*, English edition (27 June 1988), 1–2. Cf. *Origins* 18:7 (30 June 1988): 97–101.

[24] This 1 July 1988 warning is printed in *L'Osservatore Romano*, English edition (11 July 1988), 1. The pope's apostolic letter, "Ecclesia Dei" (2 July 1988) regarding Archbishop Lefebvre and his followers appears in *Origins* 18:10 (4 August 1988): 149–52.

Chapter 7—Growing With Life

[1] Karl Rahner, "Towards a Fundamental Theological Interpretation of Vatican II," in *Vatican II: The Unfinished Agenda*, ed. Lucien Richard, O.M.I., with Daniel Harrington, S.J. and John W. O'Malley, S.J., 10. This article first appeared in *Theological Studies* 40 (1979), 716–27.

[2] See Walbert Buhlman, *The Church of the Future: A Model for the Year 2000* (Maryknoll, NY: Orbis Books, 1986), 43. Idem, *The Coming of the Third Church: An Analysis of the Present and Future of the Church* (Maryknoll, NY: Orbis Books, 1978); idem, *Courage, Church!: Essays in Ecclesial Spirituality* (Maryknoll, NY: Orbis Books, 1978); idem, *The Missions on Trial* (Maryknoll, NY: Orbis Books, 1979).

[3] Pope Paul VI, "Evangelii Nuntiandi" (1975), in Austin Flannery, ed., *Vatican II: More Postconciliar Documents*, vol. 2 (Grand Rapids, MI: Wm. B. Eerdmans Publishing Co., 1982), article 20.

[4] Ibid. article 61.

[5] Ibid. article 63.

[6] Ibid. article 64.

[7] 1985 General Assembly of the Synod of Bishops, *Final Report*, section II.D.4. *Origins* 15:27 (December 19, 1985): 450.

[8] National Conference of Catholic Bishops, "To the Ends of the Earth: A Pastoral Statement on World Mission," study edition (New York: Society for the Propagation of the Faith, 1987), article 18.

[9] Ibid. article 20.

[10] Ibid. article 32.

[11] Ibid. article 44.

[12] Anne Wilson Schaef, *Women's Reality: An Emerging Female System in a White Male Society* (New York: Harper and Row, 1985), 163.

[13] Sandra Schneiders, *Women and the Word: The Gender of God in the New Testament and the Spirituality of Women* (Mahwah, NJ: Paulist Press, 1986), 27.

[14] Ibid. 28.

[15] Ibid. 31. The seven texts are: Deuteronomy 32:18 (the God who gave you birth), Isaiah 49:15 (God cherishes Israel with a mother's love), Isaiah 66:13 (God comforts Israel as a mother comforts a child), Psalm 131:2 (the psalmist relies on God like a child quieted at its mother's breast), Isaiah 63:15 and Exodus 34:6 (the word for God's compassion derives from the Hebrew word for womb), and Isaiah 42:14 (God's anguish is like that of a woman in the pangs of childbirth).

[16] *L'Osservatore Romano*, English edition (21 September 1978), 2.

[17] 1985 General Assembly of the Synod of Bishops, section I.4. *Origins* 15:27 (19 December 1985): 445.

[18] 1985 General Assembly of the Synod of Bishops, section II.C.2. *Origins* 15:27 (19 December 1985): 448.

[19] 1987 General Assembly of the Synod of Bishops, "Message to the People of God," no. 5. The two quotes that follow are from the

same section. See also, *Origins* 17:22 (12 November 1987): 387.

[20] For the pope's critique of both capitalism and communism, see *Redemptor Hominis* (1979), nos. 15–16; *Dives in Misericordia* (1980), nos. 11–12; and *Sollicitudo Rei Socialis* (1987), nos. 20–26.